Story Grammar for Elementary School

From writers of yesterday,
for writers of tomorrow,
something for today:
a story grammar book.

Story Grammar for Elementary School

A Sentence-Composing Approach—A Student Worktext

DON and JENNY KILLGALLON

HEINEMANN
Portsmouth, NH

Heinemann
361 Hanover Street
Portsmouth, NH 03801–3912
www.heinemann.com

Offices and agents throughout the world

ISBN-10: 0-325-01246-6
ISBN-13: 978-0-325-01246-9

Editor: Lisa Luedeke
Production: Elizabeth Valway
Cover design: Shawn Girsberger
Composition: House of Equations, Inc.
Manufacturing: Steve Bernier

Printed in the United States of America on acid-free paper
16 17 18   EBM   7 8

Contents

STORY GRAMMAR   1

Grammar and stories—what's the link? You'll find out here, and on every page in this worktext.

IMITATING STORY SENTENCES   2

You probably learned lots of things by watching other people do them, people who are really good at what they do. Well, who do you know who is really good at writing sentences? How about authors of famous stories? Here, you'll learn how they build their sentences, and you'll practice ways to imitate what they do, so you can build your sentences like theirs.

SENTENCE PARTS

Building good sentences is like building just about anything. You need to know the tools and how to use them. After reviewing subjects and predicates (the basics), you'll learn and practice how to build better sentences with tools used by authors of stories.

SENTENCE POSITIONS

If you're like most people, you like variety—in clothes, hairstyles, room arrangements, food, friends. One way you can vary your sentences is to learn three different places to use sentence-building tools.

WRITING STORY SENTENCES   91

Put it all together. Here, you'll review how to build better sentences with the sentence tools and positions you've practiced. You'll study how famous author J. K. Rowling uses them in the *Harry Potter* stories. Then you'll use them to build magical sentences for your own *Harry Potter* episode.

Contents

Throughout this worktext, your visible teacher team-teaches with hundreds of invisible teachers. You'll find a complete list of the invisible ones at the end of this worktext. They are the authors of the model sentences you will imitate, and they, along with your classroom teacher, are your teachers for building better sentences.

Acknowledgments

Thanks to these folks:

- Karen Pavelka, children's librarian, for recommending stories
- Joni Thorne, children's teacher, for loving the Harry Potter stories
- Kylie and Brennan Doherty, children, for their favorite stories
- *At Heinemann:* Lisa Luedeke, for her vision, and Elizabeth Valway, for her sight

Last but foremost, thanks—deep and wide—to the many authors of stories in this worktext, your invisible teachers, whose story grammar becomes sentence-composing lessons. You're about to enter their classroom.

Without grammar, there would be no sentences, and without sentences, there would be no stories. To have sentences, we need grammar, and to have stories, we need sentences. Both the story in the sentence, and the sentence in the story are taught in *Story Grammar* through sentences from hundreds of stories. Here are a few. Which do your recognize?

Harry Potter, A Series of Unfortunate Events, The Chronicles of Narnia, The Hardy Boys, Nancy Drew, Bunnicula, Charlotte's Web, Holes, There's a Boy in the Girls' Bathroom, Bridge to Terabithia, Little House on the Prairie, Jacob Have I Loved, Because of Winn-Dixie, Hoot, The Higher Power of Lucky, Harry the Dirty Dog, Charlie and the Chocolate Factory, Matilda, A Wrinkle in Time, How to Eat Fried Worms, Tales of a Fourth Grade Nothing, The Phantom Tollbooth, The High King, The Velveteen Rabbit, The Book of Three, The Secret Garden, The Wizard of Oz, The White Giraffe, The BFG, The Hobbit

When you finish *Story Grammar for Elementary School*, you'll know the same grammar used in sentences from those and other favorite stories to use in your own writing.

What are some things you learned to do by watching other people do them—like swinging a bat, making pancakes, buttoning your shirt or blouse, flying a kite, riding a bike? How did you learn these and other things? You learned probably by watching people and then imitating what they did.

You can learn how to write sentences like ones by famous authors of stories by imitating authors who know—really, really know—how to build great sentences. They include authors like Madeleine L'Engle (*A Wrinkle in Time*), Katherine Paterson (*Bridge to Terabithia*), C. S. Lewis (*The Chronicles of Narnia*), Lemony Snicket (*A Series of Unfortunate Events*), and J. K. Rowling (*Harry Potter* novels), plus many others whose sentences are in this worktext to teach you to build great sentences like theirs. Those authors are your invisible teachers.

Imitating sentences is like filling in a picture in a coloring book. When you color a picture, you're given the shape for the picture, and you add your own colors. When you imitate a sentence, you're given the shape for the sentence, and you add your own words. In the following practices, you'll learn how to imitate great sentences.

PRACTICE 1: CHUNKING

People read and write sentences one sentence part at a time. Each sentence part is a "chunk" of meaning in the sentence. Read each pair of sentences a chunk (sentence part) at a time. Choose the sentence that makes sense because it is divided into meaningful chunks.

EXAMPLE

Sentences:

a. The / idea of cutting and sewing a / dress by / herself was novel and exciting.

b. The idea / of cutting and sewing a dress / by herself / was novel and exciting.

Elizabeth George Speare, The Witch of Blackbird Pond

CORRECT: b

1a. Dessert was an over-baked / chocolate / chip cookie the size of a hockey / puck and just about as tasty.

1b. Dessert was / an over-baked chocolate chip cookie / the size of a hockey puck / and just about as tasty.

Carl Hiaasen, Hoot

2a. They now unwrapped the / blanket, and there in the center was a / tiny black / and white rabbit, sitting in a shoe box filled with / dirt.

2b. They now unwrapped the blanket, / and there in the center / was a tiny black and white rabbit, / sitting in a shoe box / filled with dirt.

Deborah and James Howe, Bunnicula: A Rabbit-Tale of Mystery

3a. On Sundays, the / park is closed to traffic, and you can ride your / bicycle all over without worrying about being / run down by / some crazy driver.

3b. On Sundays, / the park is closed to traffic, / and you can ride your bicycle all over / without worrying about being run down / by some crazy driver.

Judy Blume, Tales of a Fourth Grade Nothing

4a. To hunt the whole mountain / until the dragon / had caught the thief / and had torn and trampled him / was the dragon's one thought.

4b. To hunt the / whole mountain until / the dragon had / caught the thief and had / torn and trampled him was the dragon's one thought.

J. R. R. Tolkien, The Hobbit

5a. Otis laughed and strummed his / guitar, and the flavor of the Litmus / Lozenge opened in my mouth like a / flower blooming, all / sweet and sad.

5b. Otis laughed and strummed his guitar, / and the flavor of the Litmus Lozenge / opened in my mouth / like a flower blooming, / all sweet and sad.

Kate DiCamillo, Because of Winn-Dixie

PRACTICE 2: CHUNKING IMITATIONS

The slash marks (/) in the model divide the sentence into meaningful chunks. Copy and divide the imitation sentence into the same meaningful chunks.

EXAMPLE

MODEL: Around here, / grownups, / who are mostly real old with cats, / get mad / if dogs aren't on leashes every minute.

Beverly Cleary, Dear Mr. Henshaw

Imitation: Near home, / trucks, / which are usually very loud at night, / go fast / when cars aren't in their lanes every second.

1a. MODEL: There were bald patches / all over that pathetic dog, / places where he didn't have any fur at all.

Kate DiCamillo, Because of Winn-Dixie

1b. **Imitation:** There was a wet spot all outside the bath tub, puddles where Skip hadn't cleaned up at all.

2a. MODEL: Shaking the old woman's hand / was like holding a bunch of twigs, / but her eyes / were clear and steady.

Katherine Paterson, Jacob Have I Loved

2b. **Imitation:** Holding the stuffed rabbit was like petting a real rabbit, but its nose was hard and plastic.

3a. MODEL: Steady Eddie started / snapping his fingers, / in time with the piano and the drum, / with his toothpick in his mouth / jumping right along with his fingers.

Christopher Paul Curtis, Bud, Not Buddy

3b. **Imitation:** The lead singer began moving his body in sync with the beat and backup singers, with his microphone against his mouth bobbing right along with his movements.

4a. MODEL: Without warning, / coming as a complete and unexpected shock, / Meg felt a pressure / that she had never experienced, / as though she were being completely flattened out / by an enormous steam roller.

Madeleine L'Engle, A Wrinkle in Time

4b. **Imitation:** With a thrill, occurring from a sudden but high wave, Alfredo experienced a height that he had never reached, as if he were being totally lifted up by a powerful giant hand.

PRACTICE 3: UNSCRAMBLING IMITATIONS

Unscramble both lists of sentence parts to imitate the same model. Write out the unscrambled sentences.

EXAMPLE ─────────────────────────────────────

MODEL: There was water to draw and linen to scrub, and, everlastingly, the end-less rows of vegetables to weed and hoe.

Elizabeth George Speare, *The Witch of Blackbird Pond*

List One:

a. and trash to haul

b. and, especially, the weekly list of chores to start and complete

c. there was grass to mow

Imitation:

There was grass to mow and trash to haul, and, especially, the weekly list of chores to start and complete.

List Two:

a. and games to play

b. and, always, the exciting seasonal sports to do and enjoy

c. there were songs to hear

Imitation:

There were songs to hear and games to play, and, always, the exciting seasonal sports to do and enjoy.

───

FIRST MODEL: Tobias, the remaining member of our group, was about a hundred feet above us, floating on a nice warm current of air.

K. A. Applegate, *Animorphs: The Underground*

1a. was still a step behind us

1b. Vera

1c. the shortest girl at the dance

1d. struggling with her loose, new pair of shoes

2a. was always several laps behind us

2b. Levar

2c. the last boy in the pool

2d. complaining in that whining, baby voice of his

SECOND MODEL: Only one viewer was rapt, leaning forward in her seat, nodding at each trite sentiment, smiling while dabbing at wet eyes.

Gail Carson Levine, *Ella Enchanted*

3a. shaking at each gunshot

3b. looking out of its warren

3c. quivering when looking at burly hunters

3d. only one rabbit was safe

4a. wondering about the selection process

4b. standing quietly in their places

4c. hoping while questioning in their minds

4d. mainly short people were left

PRACTICE 4: UNSCRAMBLING TO IMITATE

Unscramble the list of sentence parts to imitate the model. Write out the unscrambled sentences. Then write your own imitation of the model using something from your imagination or from a TV show, movie, story, or book.

EXAMPLE

MODEL: While everyone scattered, I crept into my favorite hiding place, the little closet tucked under the stairs.

Jean Fritz, *Homesick: My Own Story*

Scrambled Sentence Parts:

a. a temporary tent made from a cardboard box

b. Dominic came out from the shelter

c. when the rain ended

Unscrambled Sentence: When the rain ended, Dominic came out from the shelter, a temporary tent made from a cardboard box.

Sample Imitation: After the light changed, the bus arrived at everybody's favorite restaurant, a huge building packed with hungry tourists.

1. MODEL: In the hole lived Mr. Fox and Mrs. Fox and their four small Foxes.

Roald Dahl, *Fantastic Mr. Fox*

   a. hung a blouse
   b. in the closet
   c. and several colorful skirts
   d. and a dress

2. MODEL: Twice, when the train lurched, he sat up, looking around fiercely.

Robert Lipsyte, *The Contender*

   a. walking around proudly
   b. after the audience left
   c. the actress went back
   d. later

3. MODEL: When the Boy dropped off to sleep, the Rabbit would snuggle down under the Boy's warm chin and dream.

Margery Williams, The Velveteen Rabbit

   a. and purr
   b. beside the cat's soft bed
   c. the child would sneak up
   d. when the cat curled up to snooze

4. MODEL: The darkness seemed to be pressing on their eyeballs as they stood terrified, waiting.

J. K. Rowling, Harry Potter and the Chamber of Secrets

   a. eating
   b. on their faces
   c. the sun seemed to be shining
   d. while they sat relaxed

PRACTICE 5: IMITATING SENTENCES BY AUTHORS

Copy the model and the one sentence that imitates it. Then write your own imitation of the model using something from your imagination or from a TV show, movie, story, or book.

1. MODEL: Behind Count Olaf stood the hook-handed man, who smiled and waved a hook at the youngsters.

Lemony Snicket, A Series of Unfortunate Events: The Bad Beginning

   a. When the goldfish jumped out of the pond onto the deck and was wiggling there, we found it and put it back.
   b. Running around the muddy playground were kids whose parents were talking and watching the children.
   c. Inside the house lived a kindhearted woman, who laughed and distributed cookies to the children.

2. MODEL: Janice Avery and her two mean friends would roam the playground, grabbing up hopscotch rocks, running through jump ropes, and laughing while second graders screamed.

Katherine Paterson, Bridge to Terabithia

a. After their encore, Tony and Tisha tapped their way across the stage, with their shoes clicking and their canes flying furiously to the beat of the soft-shoe dance routine.

b. Randolph Hammer and his greedy buddies would devour the dessert, slurping up chocolate ice cream, poking into each other's bowls, and burping while other diners frowned.

c. The zookeeper, surprised at the behavior of the zoo animals, decided to feed them early in an attempt to calm them down when the nasty storm made them jumpy and loud.

3. MODEL: Curled up on one of her pillows, a gray fluff of kitten yawned, showing its pink tongue, tucked its head under again, and went back to sleep.

Madeleine L'Engle, *A Wrinkle in Time*

a. Knocked down by one of his brothers, the small bundle of boy fell, dropping his basketball, forced his legs up again, and started back to play.

b. She ran into the cresting waves of the ocean, holding her breath as she went under, and felt the power of the rushing tide.

c. Ignoring the criticism of her friends, she decided to continue to wear the crazy colored hat given to her by her favorite aunt.

4. MODEL: Now began the happiest times that Caspian had ever known.

C. S. Lewis, *The Chronicles of Narnia: Prince Caspian*

a. It was the third time that she had seen her in school that week.

b. Then ended the stormiest weather that they had ever endured.

c. That was the final hour of everybody's favorite day of the entire year.

5. MODEL: Dudley, who was so large his bottom drooped over either side of the kitchen chair, grinned and turned to Harry.

J. K. Rowling, *Harry Potter and the Chamber of Secrets*

a. Harvey ran into the guy he least wanted to see, the coach of his little league baseball team who had yelled at him after the game.

b. Violet, who was so loud that her voice carried into every crevice of the kitchen, screamed and called her husband.

c. Matilda, whose mother had always taught her to listen before she spoke, was silent after the joke because she thought it was not funny.

Review: Imitating sentences by authors is like filling in colors within the lines of a coloring book. You are given the shape of the sentence, and you fill in your own words.

Preview: Next, you'll see how authors build their sentences and learn how to build yours the same way.

Subjects and Predicates

Some things just go together: burgers and fries, school and, well, homework. You almost can't have one without the other. *Story Grammar* is all about writing better sentences, and, yes, two things just go together in sentences: subjects and predicates.

A sentence tells people something about a topic. The topic is called the *subject* of the sentence. Your comment about the topic is called the *predicate*.

These are just topics (subjects), not sentences.

1. the hairy giant

2. a desktop full of computer stuff

3. little Rachel with her adorable eyes

4. playing games

5. typing slowly to make fewer mistakes

6. to save money to buy a bicycle

7. what Teagan enjoys doing after school

8. the interview with the principal by Lamar

9. the newest teenage hairstyle

10. the last round of the spelling bee

These are just comments (predicates), not sentences.

1. slid down the beanstalk

2. cluttered Troy's room

3. is in the family portrait

4. makes the time fly by

5. turned out to be a good idea

6. was why Sammy took the job

7. is snacking on fresh fruit

8. was in the newspaper

9. is weird

10. resulted in a win for our team

How do you write a complete sentence? Put the above ten topics and ten comments together to make complete sentences.

These are complete sentences because each has both a subject (topic) and a predicate (comment about that topic). Subjects are underlined once, and predicates are underlined twice.

1. The hairy giant slid down the beanstalk.
2. A desktop full of computer stuff cluttered Troy's room.
3. Little Rachel with her adorable eyes is in the family portrait.
4. Playing games makes the time fly by.
5. Typing slowly to make fewer mistakes turned out to be a good idea.
6. To save money to buy a bicycle was why Sammy took the job.
7. What Teagan enjoys doing after school is snacking on fresh fruit.
8. The interview of the principal by Lamar was in the newspaper.
9. The newest teenage hairstyle is weird.
10. The last round of the spelling bee resulted in a win for our team.

SUBJECT (Topic)	PREDICATE (Comment About the Topic)
The hairy giant	slid down the beanstalk.
A desktop full of computer stuff	cluttered Troy's room.
Little Rachel with her adorable eyes	is in the family portrait.
Playing games	makes the time fly by.
Typing slowly to make fewer mistakes	turned out to be a good idea.
To save money to buy a bicycle	was why Sammy took the job.
What Teagan enjoys doing after school	is snacking on fresh fruit.
The interview of the principal by Lamar	was in the newspaper.
The newest teenage hairstyle	is weird.
The last round of the spelling bee	resulted in a win for our team.

PRACTICE 1: MATCHING

Match the subjects and predicates to make a sentence. Write out each sentence, underlining the subject once and the predicate twice.

Subjects:

1. Four dolphins, swimming side by side, ^.
   Arthur C. Clarke, *Dolphin Island*

2. To say he was handsome ^.
   John Clarke, "The Boy Who Painted Christ Black"

3. The meat, dry-cured for the feeding of the dogs, ^.
   Marjorie Kinnan Rawlings, *The Yearling*

4. Over the last few hours, a gusting wind ^.
   Larry Weinberg, *Ghost Hotel*

5. Returning with two strips of meat for the small dragon, Eragon ^.
   Christopher Paolini, *Eragon*

Predicates:

a. hung in the smoke-house

b. would be gross exaggeration

c. had blown a good deal of loose brush down to the bottom of the hill near the little cemetery

d. found the dragon sitting on the windowsill, watching the moon

e. were pushing the raft through the water

PRACTICE 2: IDENTIFYING SUBJECTS

Sometimes sentences have more than one subject. They say something about more than one topic.

1. The fierce black eyes of the man and the laughing blue eyes of the goose girl met across the strip of swamp.
   (Two subjects—What are they?)
   Elinor Mordaunt, "The Prince and the Goose Girl"

2. Driving snow, a wind that cut like a hot knife, and darkness forced them to look for a camping place.
   (Three subjects—What are they?)

Jack London, The Call of the Wild

3. The wicked eyes, the ancient face, the fierce look, the enormous size of the two-and-a-half-ton hippo required very rapid action.
   (Four subjects—What are they?)

Leon Hugo, "My Father and the Hippopotamus"

PRACTICE 3: IDENTIFYING PREDICATES

Sometimes sentences have more than one predicate. They say more than one thing about the subject.

1. The tiny dragon lost interest in Eragon and awkwardly explored the room.
   (Two predicates—What are they?)

Christopher Paolini, Eragon

2. He felt something cold on his ankles and looked under the tablecloth and saw two more of the huge worms around his ankles.
   (Three predicates—What are they?)

Thomas Rockwell, How to Eat Fried Worms

3. One of the creatures high above the trees raised its head to listen, then flew off, picked three flowers from a tree growing near the river, and brought them over to the children.

   (Four predicates—What are they?)

Madeleine L'Engle, A Wrinkle in Time

PRACTICE 4: IDENTIFYING SUBJECTS AND PREDICATES

Sometimes sentences have more than one subject *and* more than one predicate. Those sentences say more than one thing about more than one topic.

1. She and her father unrolled the paper across the kitchen and knelt with a box of crayons between them.
   (Two subjects and two predicates—What are they?)

Beverly Cleary, Ramona and Her Father

2. The tall skinny Bean and dwarfish pot-bellied Bunce drove their machines like maniacs, raced the motors, and made the shovels dig at a terrific speed.
   (Two subjects and three predicates—What are they?)

   Roald Dahl, *Fantastic Mr. Fox*

3. The four children and the Dwarf went down to the water's edge, pushed off the boat with some difficulty, and scrambled aboard.
   (Two subjects and three predicates—What are they?)

   C. S. Lewis, *The Chronicles of Narnia: Prince Caspian*

SUBJECT FACTS
(Examples are from *Charlie and the Chocolate Factory* by Roald Dahl.)

1. Subjects can be at the very beginning of the sentence.	<u>The poor fellow</u>, looking thin and starved, was sitting there trying to eat a bowl full of mashed-up green caterpillars.
2. Subjects can be someplace else in a sentence—even at the end.	In the town, actually within sight of Charlie's house, was <u>an enormous chocolate factory</u>! *The sentence could have the subject at the beginning, too.* <u>An enormous chocolate factory</u> was in the town, actually within sight of Charlie's house. *Either way, the subject is the same—whether it's at the beginning or the end of the sentence—because it's the topic of the sentence.*
3. Subjects can be long.	<u>The one food that Oompa-Loompas longed for more than any other</u> was the cacao bean.
4. Subjects can be short.	<u>The cacao bean</u> is chocolate.
5. Subjects can do just one thing.	<u>Charlie</u> wolfed down the candy bar. *(continued)*

6. Subjects can do more than one thing.	<u>Charlie</u> grabbed the candy bar and quickly tore off the wrapper and took an enormous bite.
7. Sentences can have just one subject.	Twice a day, on his way to and from school, <u>little Charlie Bucket</u> had to walk right past the gates of the chocolate factory.
8. Sentences can have more than one subject.	<u>Lots of children</u> and <u>many grown-ups</u> pushed their ways into The Chocolate Room.
9. Sentences must have subjects—or they won't make sense!	**? (no subject)** would eat ten Oompa-Loompas for breakfast and come galloping back for a second helping. *Without a subject, we don't know who or what would eat ten Oompa-Loompas for breakfast and come galloping back for a second helping.*

PREDICATE FACTS

1. Predicates usually come after the subject.	The poor fellow, looking thin and starved, <u>was sitting there trying to eat a bowl full of mashed-up green caterpillars</u>.
2. Predicates can sometimes come before the subject.	<u>In the town, actually within sight of Charlie's house</u>, <u>was</u> an enormous chocolate factory! *Rearranged, the sentence could have the predicate after the subject.* An enormous chocolate factory <u>was in the town, actually within sight of Charlie's house</u>. *Either way, the predicate is the same—whether it's at the beginning or the end of the sentence—because it's the comment about the subject.* *(continued)*

3. Predicates can be short.	The one food that Oompa-Loompas longed for more than any other <u>was the cacao bean</u>.
4. Predicates can be long.	Charlie <u>climbed onto the bed and tried to calm the three old people who were still petrified with fear</u>.
5. Predicates can tell just one thing.	Charlie <u>wolfed down the candy bar</u>.
6. Predicates can tell more than one thing.	Charlie <u>grabbed the candy bar</u> and <u>quickly tore off the wrapper</u> and <u>took an enormous bite</u>.
7. Sentences must have predicates— or they won't make sense!	Five children and nine grown-ups ? **(no predicate)** *Without a predicate, we don't know what five children and nine grown-ups did.*

Review: Every sentence has at least one subject and at least one predicate.

Preview: Tools added to the subject or to the predicate or to both build good sentences. Now you'll learn the tools you need to build better sentences.

Tools

All sentences need a subject and a predicate, but good sentences usually have something else: *tools*, which are sentence parts of different shapes and sizes that you'll learn and practice here by seeing how authors use them to build great sentences. You'll then have a toolbox of your own for building great sentences.

Tools add details and dazzle to make sentences more interesting. Below are pairs of sentences. Subjects are underlined once. Predicates are underlined twice. Tools are **bold**.

The first sentence, without tools, is plain. The second sentence, with tools, the one the author actually wrote, is more interesting and stylish.

1a. The Mole had been working very hard all the morning.

1b. The Mole had been working very hard all the morning, **spring-cleaning his little home**.

> Kenneth Grahame, *The Wind in the Willows*

2a. The handle was ivory.

2b. The handle was ivory, **circled with gold that wound its way to the end and then formed the shape of a scorpion**.

> Walter Dean Myers, *Legend of Tarik*

3a. The Big Friendly Giant had picked her up off the table and popped her into his waistcoat pocket.

3b. **Before Sophie could protest,** the Big Friendly Giant had picked her up off the table and popped her into his waistcoat pocket.

> Roald Dahl, *The BFG*

4a. Stanley thought about his great-grandfather.

4b. **Walking across the desolate wasteland,** Stanley thought about his great-grandfather, **the guy who was robbed by Kissin' Kate Barlow**.

> Louis Sachar, *Holes*

5a. I crept into my favorite hiding place.

5b. **While everyone scattered,** I crept into my favorite hiding place, **the little closet tucked under the stairs**.

> Jean Fritz, *Homesick: My Own Story*

6a. <u>Sandy and Dennis</u> <u>were disgusted</u>.

6b. <u>Sandy and Dennis</u>, **her ten-year-old twin brothers, who got home from school an hour earlier than she did,** <u>were disgusted</u>.

Madeleine L'Engle, A Wrinkle in Time

7a. <u>Ima Dean</u> <u>was sitting on the floor</u>.

7b. <u>Ima Dean</u>, **with a huge bag of yellow and red wrapped candies,** <u>was sitting on the floor</u>, **delving into it, making one big pile and three smaller ones.**

Bill and Vera Cleaver, Where the Lilies Bloom

8a. <u>The four boys</u> <u>began talking at once</u>.

8b. <u>The four boys</u> <u>began talking at once</u>, **accusing, recounting, explaining.**

Thomas Rockwell, How to Eat Fried Worms

9a. <u>We</u> <u>hastened along the invisible road</u>.

9b. **Quiet, frightened, and wishing just to dump T. J. on his front porch and get back to the safety of our own beds,** <u>we</u> <u>hastened along the invisible road</u>, **brightened only by the round of the flashlight.**

Mildred D. Taylor, Roll of Thunder, Hear My Cry

10a. <u>She</u> <u>noticed very soon one little girl</u>.

10b. **On that first morning, when Sara sat at Miss Munchkin's side, aware that the whole schoolroom was devoting itself to observing her,** <u>she</u> <u>noticed very soon one little girl</u>, **about her own age, who looked at her very hard with a pair of light, rather dull, blue eyes.**

Frances Hodgson Burnett, A Little Princess

Question: What two sentence parts cannot be removed without destroying the sentence?

Answer: Subject and predicate. Take out either, and the sentence is dead.

By the way, tools can be removed, but nobody would want to because they're often the best sentence parts!

PRACTICE 1: IDENTIFYING SENTENCE PARTS

What is the bold sentence part—a subject, a predicate, or a tool?

1. Slowly, filled with dissatisfaction, he **went to his room to go to bed.**

   Betsy Byars, *The Summer of the Swans*

2. **Gasping from shortness of breath**, Mafatu raised his head and looked about.

   Armstrong Sperry, *Call It Courage*

3. The Big Friendly Giant took out a book, **very old and tattered.**

   Roald Dahl, *The BFG*

4. **Hurting her** made me hurt.

   Rosa Guy, *Edith Jackson*

5. Only one daughter had been born to him, **who from her cradle was called Vasilissa the Beautiful.**

   Post Wheeler, "Vasilissa the Beautiful"

6. **Ready**, he moved back into the tunnel, taking a position beyond the puddle so that he was almost in darkness.

   Robb White, *Deathwatch*

7. I **pressed my back against the tunnel wall**, still holding Terri's hand.

   R. L. Stine, *Ghost Beach*

8. **An old woman** stepped out of the kitchen, wiping her hands on an apron.

   Kate DiCamillo, *The Miraculous Journey of Edward Tulane*

9. Turning away, he gathered several more sticks of firewood and, **in silence**, put them on the wagon.

   Mildred D. Taylor, *Let the Circle Be Unbroken*

10. Then, as quickly as it had become a tiger, the ghost **changed into a man with the face of a rat**.

Walter Dean Myers, Legend of Tarik

Directions: Sentences 11–15 have three bold sentence parts. Tell what kind for each: *subject, predicate,* or *tool.* Sometimes it's just one kind, sometimes two kinds, sometimes all three.

11. (A) **With rattlesnake speed,** (B) **Maniac** (C) **snatched the book back.**

Jerry Spinelli, Maniac Magee

12. He (A) **got up,** shivering in the chilly dawn, (B) **cooked a breakfast of pancakes and the last of his bacon,** and (C) **closed his pack.**

Hal Borland, When the Legends Die

13. One of the baby swans, (A) **more daring than the others,** (B) **left the nest** and (C) **teetered around on the shore of the little island.**

E. B. White, The Trumpet of the Swan

14. (A) **With two or three deft motions,** Carlos (B) **flattened the cartons** and (C) **stacked them carefully on his pushcart.**

Jean Merrill, The Pushcart War

15. (A) **Mrs. Rachel,** (B) **before she closed the door,** (C) **took mental note of everything on that table.**

L. M. Montgomery, Anne of Green Gables

PRACTICE 2: MATCHING

Match the subjects and their predicates with the tools to make a better sentence with more information. Write out each sentence, inserting the tools at the caret (^).

Subjects and Predicates:

Tools:

1. An owl screeched, ^.
   Christopher Paolini, *Eragon*

   a. cutting through the silence

2. Templeton, ^, heard the commotion and awoke.
   E. B. White, *Charlotte's Web*

   b. throwing back his head

3. ^, Stuart was often hard to find around the house.
   E. B. White, *Stuart Little*

   c. because he was so small

4. The old witch ate it, ^.
   Post Wheeler, "Vasilissa the Beautiful"

   d. bones and all, almost to the last morsel, enough for four strong men

5. ^, Billy dropped the squirming night crawler into his mouth and chewed and chewed.
   Thomas Rockwell, *How to Eat Fried Worms*

   e. asleep in the straw

PRACTICE 3: UNSCRAMBLING TO IMITATE

In the model and the scrambled list, tell what part is the subject, what part is the predicate, and what part is the tool. Unscramble and write out the sentence parts to imitate the model, including punctuation. Then write your own imitation using something from your imagination or from a TV show, movie, story, or book.

1. MODEL: Nobody said a word, waiting.
   Cynthia Rylant, *Missing May*

   a. smiling
   b. sang a song
   c. everyone

2. MODEL: Mrs. Salt and Mrs. Teavee, the only women now left in the party, were getting very out of breath.

Roald Dahl, *Charlie and the Chocolate Factory*

a. Zee and Dominic
b. were feeling very out of touch
c. the only boys still part of the band

3. MODEL: Choking back his fear, Taran leaped to his feet and plunged into the undergrowth.

Lloyd Alexander, *The Book of Three*

a. reached for the kitten and hoped for its rescue
b. climbing under the porch
c. Molly

4. MODEL: Laughter, loud and warm from their long and intimate relationship, filled the room.

Rosa Guy, *The Friends*

a. pink and squirmy from the dark and fertile dirt
b. filled the can
c. worms

5. MODEL: Matilda was curled up in an armchair in a corner, totally absorbed in a book.

Roald Dahl, *Matilda*

a. was bending over the television in the den
b. Al
c. completely focused on the problem

6. MODEL: A tuna fish, fierce and very hungry, came darting through the waves.

Leo Lionni, "Swimmy"

a. crept down our sidewalk
b. a scary cat
c. black and very slow

7. MODEL: Jodi slept, curled up in back with her stuffed animal friend.

   Donna Hill, "Ghost Cat"

   a. seated on the bench with his bandaged swollen hand
   b. moaned
   c. Ricky

8. MODEL: Little Man, a very small six-year-old and a most finicky dresser, brushed his hair.

   Mildred D. Taylor, *Song of the Trees*

   a. started her project
   b. Shea
   c. a very clever thirteen-year-old and an always excellent student

9. MODEL: They went home, to rest, to eat beans and chili, to wait for spring and a new season.

   Hal Borland, *When the Legends Die*

   a. drew pictures
   b. we
   c. to use pastels and charcoal, to sketch for fun and a new hobby

10. MODEL: The twins, who had finished their homework, were allowed to watch half an hour of TV.

    Madeleine L'Engle, *A Wrinkle in Time*

    a. was starting to make a ball of sleeping fur
    b. who had lapped up its milk
    c. the kitten

PRACTICE 4: ADDING TOOLS

At each caret mark (^), add a tool. Blend your new information with the rest of the sentence. Make your tools different shapes and sizes, but don't add complete sentences, only sentence parts.

1. Lavinia Nebbs walked down the midnight street, ^.

   Ray Bradbury, "The Whole Town's Sleeping"

2. ^, she would have to practice every day.

   Eleanor Coerr, *Sadako and the Thousand Paper Cranes*

3. The third girl, ^, used an eyebrow pencil to give herself a heavy brow.

   Beverly Cleary, *Ramona and Her Father*

4. ^, she heard voices.

   Lauren St. John, *The White Giraffe*

5. Dad talked Mom into naming the baby after one of his favorite writers, ^.

   Carl Hiaasen, *Flush*

6. Steven, ^, had gone into a kind of shock.

   Gary Paulsen, *The Tent*

7. ^, Stuart grew more and more nervous.

   E. B. White, *Stuart Little*

8. ^, ^, Tarren drove up. *(Add two tools.)*

   Judy Blume, *Here's to You, Rachel Robinson*

9. Papa sat on a bench in the barn, ^, ^. *(Add two tools.)*

   Mildred D. Taylor, *Roll of Thunder, Hear My Cry*

10. ^, ^, the biggest rat she had ever seen appeared. *(Add two tools.)*

   Robert C. O'Brien, *Mrs. Frisby and the Rats of NIMH*

Let's review the importance of tools in building better sentences. Take a look at these sentences from E. B. White's classic story *Charlotte's Web*, first without tools, then with tools the author used.

Without Tools: These are sentences with just a subject and its predicate.

With Tools: These are much better sentences with tools that add detail and dazzle.

1a. She just sat there.

1b. She just sat there, **thinking what a blissful world it was and how lucky she was to have entire charge of a pig.**

2a. It's hard to sleep.

2b. **When your stomach is empty and your mind is full**, it's hard to sleep.

3a. He felt relieved.

3b. **When he looked up and saw Mr. Zuckerman standing quite close to him holding a pail of warm slops,** he felt relieved.

4a. Wilbur the pig amused himself in the mud.

4b. **While the children swam and played and splashed water at each other,** Wilbur the pig amused himself in the mud, **along the edge of the brook, where it was warm and moist and delightfully sticky and oozy.**

5a. Ants crawled.

5b. **For several days and several nights,** ants crawled, **here and there, up and down, around and about, waving at Wilbur, trailing tiny draglines behind them, and exploring their home.**

Without tools, sentences are just skeletons, dead and dry, going nowhere. Sentences with tools put meat and muscle on those useless bare bones to give them life and power. These sentences go anywhere.

Give life and muscle to your sentences by using the three kinds of tools of authors like E. B. White.

Kinds of Tools

Sentence-building tools come in three kinds: ***words, phrases, clauses.***

1. *Words* are the shortest of the sentence-building tools, because they're, well, just words.

2. *Phrases* are groups of words.

3. *Clauses* are also groups of words, but clauses contain a subject and its predicate. Phrases don't contain a subject and predicate.

There are two kinds of clauses: *independent* and *dependent.* Here's the difference.

An independent clause can be a sentence:

Example of Independent Clause: The grasshopper jumped six feet.

A dependent clause cannot be a sentence because it is only a sentence part:

Examples of Dependent Clauses:

1. because the grasshopper jumped six feet

   or

2. which jumped six feet

In the first dependent clause, readers don't know what happened because the grasshopper jumped six feet. In the second dependent clause, readers don't know what the word *which* means—because it could refer to anyone or anything that can jump six feet!

To make complete sense, a dependent clause must be joined to an independent clause within the same sentence. A dependent clause depends on an independent clause for meaning, just as a child depends on adults for care.

Although a dependent clause is a sentence part and not a complete sentence, it is a valuable tool for adding information to sentences.

Example:

Because the grasshopper jumped six feet, the judges made it the winner of the annual grasshopper contest.

   or

The judges made the grasshopper, *which jumped six feet*, the winner of the annual grasshopper contest.

In both examples, the independent clause is *the judges made it the winner of the annual grasshopper contest.*

PRACTICE 5: IDENTIFYING CLAUSES

Sentences below are arranged as lists of clauses. For each clause, tell the kind: independent or dependent. Ignore <u>underlined</u> words (*and, but, so*) that connect clauses but aren't part of those clauses.

EXAMPLE

(A) She waved her hand to land a mock spank on Gilly's bottom, <u>but</u>

(B) after her hand swept the air,

(C) Gilly's bottom along with the rest of her was well down the hall.

Katherine Paterson, *The Great Gilly Hopkins*

Answers:

(A) independent clause, (B) dependent clause, (C) independent clause

Hint: An easy way to tell the difference between independent clauses and dependent clauses is to look at the first word. If it's one of these words, it's a dependent clause:

after, although, as, before, because, how, if, since, that, though, until, what, when, where, which, while, who, whom, whose, why

Memorize them.

---

1. (A) As they entered the building,
   (B) Sadako felt a pang of fear.

   Eleanor Coerr, *Sadako and the Thousand Paper Cranes*

2. (A) He lives in a great, big, desolate old house in the country, <u>and</u>
   (B) no one goes near him.

   Frances Hodgson Burnett, *The Secret Garden*

3. (A) All the eyes of Paris were fixed on the Eiffel Tower,
   (B) which slowly drooped over like soft rubber.

   Chris Van Allsburg, *The Sweetest Fig*

4. (A) My tongue was swollen and sore from drinking scalding-hot tea, <u>and</u>
   (B) the tip of my nose ached from frostbite.

   Richard E. Byrd, *Alone*

5. (A) After Mrs. Mallard had laid eight eggs in the nest,
   (B) she couldn't go to visit Michael any more,
   (C) because she had to sit on the eggs to keep them warm.

   Robert McCloskey, "Make Way for Ducklings"

6. (A) All in all, he thought everyone would be much happier
   (B) if he sat in the closet, <u>but</u>,
   (C) unfortunately, his desk didn't fit.

   Louis Sachar, *There's a Boy in the Girls' Bathroom*

7. (A) The museum restaurant wouldn't open until eleven-thirty, <u>and</u>
   (B) the snack bar wouldn't open until after that, <u>so</u>
   (C) they left the museum to get breakfast.

   E. L. Konigsburg, *From the Mixed-up Files of Mrs. Basil E. Frankweiler*

8. (A) I was just fourteen years of age
   (B) when a coward going by the name of Tom Chaney shot my father down in Fort Smith, Arkansas, and robbed him of his life and his horse and $150 in cash money plus two California gold pieces,
   (C) which he carried in his trouser band.

   Charles Portis, *True Grit*

9. (A) When the seal was dead,
   (B) the bear attended first to herself and got rid of the wet from her coat
   (C) before it could freeze.

   Norah Burke, "Polar Night"

10. (A) He was a small boy of six
    (B) who lived just around the corner from her, <u>and</u>
    (C) for days he had been going on about this great talking parrot.

    Roald Dahl, *Matilda*

PRACTICE 6: TELLING THE KIND OF TOOL

Sentences below are arranged as lists of sentence parts. For each part, tell the kind of tool: *word, phrase, dependent clause, independent clause.* Ignore <u>underlined</u> words (*and, but*) that connect clauses but aren't part of those clauses.

EXAMPLE

(A) Slowly,

(B) filled with dissatisfaction,

(C) he went to his room to go to bed

(D) because he was tired.

Betsy Byars, *The Summer of the Swans*

Answers: (A) word, (B) phrase, (C) independent clause, (D) dependent clause

1. (A) His voice seemed sad,
    (B) although he was trying to be cheerful.

    Theodore Taylor, *The Cay*

2. (A) They all saw it this time,
    (B) a whiskered furry face
    (C) which had looked out at them from behind a tree.

    C. S. Lewis, *The Chronicles of Narnia: The Lion, the Witch, and the Wardrobe*

3. (A) After the other children had disappeared,
    (B) she remained at her desk,
    (C) quiet <u>and</u>
    (D) thoughtful.

    Roald Dahl, *Matilda*

4. (A) First snow came,
    (B) six inches of it in the night,
    (C) fluffy
    (D) as cotton.

    Hal Borland, *When the Legends Die*

5. (A) Not daring to turn her head,
    (B) from a corner of her eye
    (C) she grew aware of a strange, humped shadow,
    (D) motionless.

    Lloyd Alexander, *The High King*

6. (A) Leslie loaned Jess all of her books about Narnia
    (B) because she wanted him to know important ideas:
    (C) how things went in a magic kingdom,
    (D) how the animals and the trees must be protected, <u>and</u>
    (E) how a ruler must behave.

    Katherine Paterson, *Bridge to Terabithia*

7. (A) Dizzy <u>and</u>
    (B) bruised,
    (C) covered in soot,

(D) he got gingerly to his feet,

(E) holding his broken glasses up to his eyes.

J. K. Rowling, *Harry Potter and the Chamber of Secrets*

8. (A) Taking the potion,

(B) the young man drank it in a single gulp and fell into a deep sleep, <u>and</u>

(C) for twenty-four hours

(D) the girl sat by his side,

(E) watching over him,

(F) while the magic drained out of him.

Winifred Finlay, "The Water-Horse of Barra"

9. (A) As the door opened,

(B) Fortinbras streaked in,

(C) panting from exhaustion,

(D) wet <u>and</u>

(E) shiny

(F) as a seal.

Madeleine L'Engle, *A Wrinkle in Time*

10. (A) Luckily,

(B) the whole head and jaws of the dragon could not squeeze into the cave, <u>but</u>

(C) the nostrils sent forth fire and vapor to pursue him, <u>and</u>

(D) he was nearly overcome

(E) as he stumbled blindly on in great pain and fear,

(F) in dreadful agony.

J. R. R. Tolkien, *The Hobbit*

PRACTICE 7: IMITATING SENTENCES BY AUTHORS

Write an imitation of each model sentence. Then choose one of your imitations to read to the class to see if your classmates can guess your model.

1. MODEL: The toothpaste factory, the place where Mr. Bucket worked, suddenly went bust and had to close down.

Roald Dahl, *Charlie and the Chocolate Factory*

Sample: The restless horse, the animal that Toni loved, eventually became quiet and began to settle down.

2. MODEL: Disappointed, Taran hastened to catch up with Gwydion.

   Lloyd Alexander, *The Book of Three*

   Sample: Excited, Mary began to run up to the pony.

3. MODEL: Jonas's father, wearing his nurturing uniform, entered the room, cradling a tiny child in a soft blanket in his arms.

   Lois Lowry, *The Giver*

   Sample: Little Sam, holding a pizza slice, approached the salad bar, placing a clean bowl on the tray for his food.

4. MODEL: The house was before them, overgrown with honeysuckle, dark, looking abandoned.

   Cynthia Voigt, *Homecoming*

   Sample: A desk was near him, covered with junk, messy, looking awful.

5. MODEL: It appeared in the dusk as a crouched and shadowy animal, silent, gloomy, capable.

   Edmund Ware, "An Underground Episode"

   Sample: The quarterback ran down the field like a mad and speeding tiger, fierce, aggressive, triumphant.

PRACTICE 8: REVIEWING THE TOOLS

Below are sentences with words, phrases, or dependent clauses omitted at the caret mark (^). Add the kind of sentence-building tool indicated.

Add a Word:

1. ^, she limped across the room and sat in her chair by the window.

   Eleanor Coerr, *Sadako and the Thousand Paper Cranes*

2. When the bell rang for recess, he put on his red jacket and walked outside, ^.

   Louis Sachar, *There's a Boy in the Girls' Bathroom*

3. Charles Wallace began to speak, ^, with none of the usual baby preliminaries, using entire sentences.

   Madeleine L'Engle, *A Wrinkle in Time*

4. ^, in a house on Egypt Street, there lived a rabbit who was made almost entirely of china.

    Kate DiCamillo, *The Miraculous Journey of Edward Tulane*

5. ^, Thomas ate two portions of meat, nothing else.

    Hal Borland, *When the Legends Die*

Add a Phrase:

6. Henry, ^, is always making jokes about me and Sheila.

    Judy Blume, *Tales of a Fourth Grade Nothing*

7. The bear was charging across the shallows in the creek and knocking up sheets of water high in the bright sun, charging with her fur up and her long teeth bared, ^.

    Fred Gipson, *Old Yeller*

8. ^, Jody knew that the pony was worse, with eyes closed and sealed shut with dried mucus.

    John Steinbeck, *The Red Pony*

9. Rosalind had never seen so many clothes in one place, ^.

    Jeanne Birdsall, *The Penderwicks*

10. A chill ran down my spine as I looked behind me and saw one of the lions leisurely sauntering down into the moat , ^.

    Jack Prelutsky, "A Day at the Zoo"

Add a Dependent Clause:

11. ^, the phone rang, and since Mrs. Quimby was standing near it, she answered.

    Beverly Cleary, *Ramona Forever*

12. From behind Bilbo came the great spider, who had been busy tying Bilbo up ^.

    J. R. R. Tolkien, *The Hobbit*

13. Little Nutbrown Hare, ^, held on tight to Big Nutbrown Hare's very long ears.

    Sam McBratney, "Guess How Much I Love You"

14. The truck drivers, ^, were furious.

Jean Merrill, The Pushcart War

15. ^, he found Ron being violently sick in the pumpkin patch.

J. K. Rowling, Harry Potter and the Chamber of Secrets

STORY GRAMMAR

Using one of the authors' sentences as a starter sentence, write the opening paragraph of a story. The complete story will take lots of pages to tell, but your job is <u>to write just the first paragraph, at least five sentences long</u>. Write your sentences so well that the author of your starter sentence would say, "Great job!"

■ Just as the authors' sentences use tools to build their sentences, within your paragraph use *tools to make your paragraph sparkle and shine*. For your tools, use at least one word, one phrase, one dependent clause.

■ Exchange your rough draft with drafts of other students in your class to get suggestions for improvement. Use suggestions to revise your paragraph to make it better.

■ Publish your writing by reading your paragraph to the class or posting it online. See how other students who used your same first sentence wrote their first paragraphs to begin that long story.

Tools Are **Bold:**

1. **Since my childhood feels like a story**, I decided to tell it that way, **letting the events fall as they would into the shape of a story.**

Jean Fritz, Homesick: My Own Story

2. I went very slowly, **because I had to crawl on my hands and knees, carrying the food tied to my back**, and **dragging the weapons.**

Scott O'Dell, Island of the Blue Dolphins

3. **Wildly**, Alfred bolted across the street, **sidestepping a taxicab by inches, ignoring the horns and curses of braking drivers**.

Robert Lipsyte, The Contender

4. **High up on the long hill they called the Saddle Back, behind the ranch and the county road,** the boy sat on his horse, **facing east, with his eyes dazzled by the rising sun.**

   Mary O'Hara, *My Friend Flicka*

5. **Sometimes now, in the hush of night, when the moon was full and the light lay in silver bands across the pandanus mats, and all the village was sleeping,** Mafatu awoke and sat upright.

   Armstrong Sperry, *Call It Courage*

Tip for Better Revising: Always, when you revise something you've written, look for places to use tools to add detail and dazzle to your writing.

Review: There are three kinds of sentence parts: *subjects, predicates,* and *tools*. Tools add detail and dazzle to sentences. There are three kinds of tools: *words, phrases,* or *dependent clauses.*

TOOL FACTS
(Examples are from *Charlie and the Chocolate Factory* by Roald Dahl.)

1. A tool can be at the very beginning of the sentence.	<u>Looking thin and starved</u>, the poor fellow was sitting there trying to eat a bowl full of mashed-up green caterpillars.
2. A tool can be at the very end of the sentence.	The old people in the bed all leaned forward, <u>craning their scraggy necks</u>.
3. A tool can be somewhere in-between the beginning and the end of the sentence.	Mrs. Salt and Mrs. Teavee, <u>the only women now left in the party</u>, were getting very out of breath.
4. A tool can be a word.	Little Charlie sat very still on the edge of the bed, <u>staring</u>.
5. A tool can be a phrase.	It was a very beautiful thing, <u>this Golden Ticket</u>.
6. A tool can be a dependent clause.	<u>As the gates closed with a clang</u>, all sight of the outside world disappeared. *(continued)*

7. Sentences can have more than one tool.	<u>While they were talking</u>, Mr. and Mrs. Bucket, <u>Charlie's mother and father</u>, had come quietly into the room, and now were standing just inside the door, <u>listening</u>.

Preview: Next you'll review everything you've learned about sentence parts (*subjects, predicates,* and *tools*) through sentences from Lemony Snicket's *A Series of Unfortunate Events: The Bad Beginning*.

Reviewing Sentence Parts

A Series of Unfortunate Events: The Bad Beginning by Lemony Snicket

The First Story in the Series

Lemony Snicket wrote thirteen novels (long stories) called *A Series of Unfortunate Events*. The first novel is called *The Bad Beginning*. Here's the opening of the story:

> If you are interested in stories with happy endings, you would be better off reading some other book. In this book, not only is there no happy ending, there is no happy beginning and very few happy things in the middle. This is because not very many happy things happen in the lives of the three Baudelaire orphans. Violet, Klaus, and Sunny Baudelaire were intelligent children, and they were charming, and resourceful, and had pleasant facial features, but they were extremely unlucky, and most everything that happened to them was rife with misfortune, misery, and despair. I'm sorry to tell you this, but that is how the story goes.

The rest of the story, like all thirteen of the Lemony Snicket stories, is about the "series of unfortunate events" that happen to three orphaned siblings—Violet, Klaus, and the baby, Sunny—when they are placed in the care of the evil Count Olaf.

The Grammar

The author of the miserable events that befall the children is a very good writer, with very well-built sentences. In these activities, you will read many of his sentences—from the first book in the series, and, later in this worktext, from the last book. You'll learn how to imitate Lemony's sentences. Then you'll write your own sentences built like his.

By the way, "Lemony Snicket" is not the author's real name; it is a made-up one called a *pen name*, chosen perhaps because it's funny and memorable. Why don't you make up a pen name for yourself? Here are some other pen names:

PEN NAME	REAL NAME
Mark Twain, *Tom Sawyer*	Samuel Clemmens
Lewis Carroll, *Alice's Adventures in Wonderland*	Charles Dodgson
Lemony Snicket, *A Series of Unfortunate Events*	Daniel Handler
J. K. Rowling, *Harry Potter* series	Joanne Rowling

REVIEW 1: SUBJECTS, PREDICATES, TOOLS

Tell what's missing—a subject, a predicate, or a tool. Then pretend you are Lemony Snicket and add what's missing. **Important:** Make your tools different shapes and sizes, but don't add complete sentences, because tools are sentence parts, not sentences.

EXAMPLE

1. Then, leaving Sunny behind in the kitchen, ^ walked into the dining room.

   Sample Subject: Klaus with the dishes

2. Violet, with some embarrassment, ^.

   Sample Predicate: pretended after lunch it was not her stomach making growling sounds

3. Violet stood up and walked out of the room, ^.

   Sample Tool: sick from the troll drooling over its food and making disgusting gurgles

---

1. Klaus Baudelaire, the middle child, and the only boy, ^.
2. ^ just sat there, stunned, scared.
3. ^, the children put away the clean oatmeal bowls in the kitchen cupboards, which watched them with painted eyes.
4. Klaus, the biggest reader of the three children, a very smart lad, ^.
5. ^ walked slowly to the front door and peered through the peephole, which was in the shape of an eye.
6. As Violet spoke, ^ reached into his pocket for his handkerchief, covering his mouth, and coughed many, many times into it.
7. ^, the book you are holding in your hands does not have a happy ending.
8. The Baudelaire parents had an enormous library in their mansion, ^.
9. Biting down on her hand to keep from crying out in pain, Violet ^.
10. The entire house of Count Olaf sagged to the side, ^.

REVIEW 2: WORDS, PHRASES, DEPENDENT CLAUSES

Each sentence is missing a word, a phrase, or a dependent clause. Pretend you are Lemony Snicket and add what's missing.

EXAMPLE

1. **Add a Word:** Violet, ^, gave the rope a good yank.

   Sample: worried

2. **Add a Phrase:** Violet knelt at Klaus's side, ^.

   Sample: helping him to recover from the blow to his head from the tyrannical troll in the attic

3. **Add a Dependent Clause:** ^, Violet stroked Sunny's hair, murmuring that everything was all right.

   Sample: As Sunny's sobbing grew softer after the scare from Count Olaf

Add a Word:

1. Violet, Klaus, and Sunny looked at one another, ^.

2. Their parents had died, ^.

3. ^, Violet and Klaus would speak to each other.

Add a Phrase:

4. Sunny was very small for her age, ^.

5. ^, Violet looked like a ghost in her white wedding gown, moving slowly across the stage.

6. Violet then went over to the cardboard box and took out the ugliest of the clothes that Mrs. Poe had purchased, ^.

Add a Dependent Clause:

7. Violet, Klaus, and Sunny continued weeping ^.

8. Violet, ^, immediately got out of bed and went to the cardboard box to find some proper clothing.

9. Behind Count Olaf stood the hook-handed man, ^.

10. If you are literally jumping for joy, it means you are leaping in the air ^.

REVIEW 3: IMITATING SNICKETY SENTENCES

The model sentences below contain the tools you just reviewed. Copy each model sentence and its imitation. Then write your own imitation of the same model. Great! You're writing like famous author Lemony Snicket!

GROUP ONE: Model Sentences

1. Klaus felt an icy chill go through him as the horrible man spoke.

2. Violet, who usually moved slowly in the morning, nodded and immediately got out of bed and went to the cardboard box to find some proper clothing.

3. Using one of the rocks Olaf left in a pile in the corner, she broke the curtain rod into two pieces.

4. As the first light of morning trickled into the tower room, Violet reflected on all the awful things she and her siblings had experienced recently.

5. In my room, I have gathered a collection of objects that is important to me, including a dusty accordion on which I can play a few sad songs, a large bundle of notes on the activities of the orphans in this story, and a blurry photograph of a woman named Beatrice.

GROUP ONE: Imitations

A. As the last day of summer dawned over the vacationing children, they thought about all the wonderful things they and their friends had enjoyed daily.

B. In my attic, I have hung a collection of clothes that is interesting to me, including a Hawaiian muumuu in which I can dance a few hula steps, a long gown of lace with a trimming of satin along the neck, and a silk shawl from a lady named Gabriella.

C. Danny, who often performed poorly in the classroom, listened and calmly got out of his seat and went to the front board to write a dazzling sentence.

D. Tamara saw a young child run past her as the pouring rain began.

E. Holding one of the kittens its mother abandoned in a corner of the barn, she begged her own sympathetic mom with calculated pleas.

GROUP TWO: Model Sentences

6. Sunny took Justice Strauss's hand and bit it, gently.

7. Nervously, Violet gave the rope a good yank, and it stayed put.

8. Violet and Klaus read the note as they ate their breakfast, which was a gray and lumpy oatmeal Count Olaf left for them each morning in a large pot on the stove.

9. With his other hand, Count Olaf twirled his harpoon gun, a terrible weapon that had one last sharp harpoon.

10. To make a bed for Sunny, Violet removed the dusty curtains from the curtain rod that hung over the bedroom's one window and bunched them together to form a sort of cushion for her little sister.

GROUP TWO: Imitations

F. At the front door, Aunt Edna welcomed her youngest niece, a petite girl who carried a small fragrant bouquet.

G. To begin the lunch for Fred, Suzie retrieved the soup from the closest cabinet that stood near the kitchen's oak table and opened it up to start a series of steps for her brother's meal.

H. Regrettably, Schwartz told the audience a bad joke, but they laughed politely.

I. Harry lifted Mr. Brown's vase and held it, carefully.

J. Don and Jenny counted their blessings when they saw their garden, which was a colorful and happy space Don created for them every summer after a million trips to the nursery.

Building Better Sentences

The paragraph below is based upon an incident in Lemony Snicket's *The Bad Beginning*: Violet attempts to rescue her little sister, Sunny, from imprisonment in a cell in a high tower. The sentences in the paragraph are ordinary, without detail or dazzle. You can make them much, much better.

Here's how. At each caret mark (^), add a tool to make each sentence more detailed and dazzling, like the sentences in Lemony Snicket's story. For the tools you add, choose what would work best—a word, a phrase, or a dependent clause.

"The Rescue from the Tower"
1. ^, Violet needed something to use to climb the outside of the tower.
2. She thought of making a rope out of old clothes, ^.
3. ^, she attached an iron hook to the end of the rope, ^.
4. She threw it as high as she could, ^, toward the top of the tower wall.
5. ^, it fell back to the ground.
6. She threw it again, ^.
7. It fell again, ^.
8. ^, she heard it catch onto something, ^.
9. This time, ^, it stayed put.
10. Violet used the rope, ^, to climb up to rescue her little sister Sunny, ^.

Review: Words, phrases, and dependent clauses are the tools that build better sentences by adding detail and dazzle.

Preview: Authors use those tools in three places within their sentences. You'll now learn those three places to use tools to build good sentences, using this worktext as your owner's manual.

Do you like to move things around now and then, maybe rearrange your collection of music or movies, change the furniture in your room, put your clothes in different places in the closet? Why do we like to put things in new places? Maybe because they're more interesting or useful there, more convenient, more attractive, easier to get to. There are lots of reasons.

Authors do something similar with their sentences, varying where they put tools, which are the sentence parts that add dazzle and detail to sentences. Those tools—words, phrases, or dependent clauses—can be moved around within sentences, just like furniture in your room.

Your bed in your room isn't nailed to the floor, right? Well, neither are most words, phrases, and dependent clauses glued to just one place in a sentence. Just as you can move your bed around to find a better place, so can authors move their sentence parts around to get them just right.

However, there are not a million places to move a bed, only a few. You can't put it on the ceiling, so don't try! You can put it against one of the four walls, but not the one with a door in it unless you are barricading yourself from an alien from outer space with two mouths where its eyes should be, and two eyes where its ears should be, and two ears where its hands should be—you get the horrible picture.

With sentences, you have just three choices for placing sentence parts: the beginning, called an *opener*; between a subject and its verb, called an *S-V split*; and the end, called a *closer*.

Good writers use all three positions. You can, too. It's a good thing to know how to move things around to put them in better places, including sentence parts—and beds against doors in case of alien invaders.

Opener

Some things are better up front. An umbrella near the front door is handier than one in the attic. A ticket for a front-row seat to a game or concert, movie or play is better than a seat way, way back. Sometimes authors use tools at the front of the sentence to put information right away, with no delay, because it's important. Take a look at sentences without a tool up front, and then compare them to sentences with a tool up front called an *opener* because it comes at the opening of the sentence:

1. A terrible thing happened.
2. A band of wild ponies swept into the natural grazing ground.
3. He ran to the tree.
4. He couldn't imagine needing anything on earth.
5. She found tucked away under the coverlet her old crumpled straw hat.

There's not much detail or dazzle in those sentences. Now look at how the authors actually wrote their sentences, this time with *openers*:

1. **Because of my grandfather's bragging, and his firm belief in my dogs and me**, a terrible thing happened.
   Wilson Rawls, *Where the Red Fern Grows*

2. **With manes and tails flying**, a band of wild ponies swept into the natural grazing ground.
   Marguerite Henry, *Misty of Chincoteague*

3. **Setting down his lilies carefully on the grass**, he ran to the tree.
   J. R. R. Tolkien, *The Lord of the Rings: The Fellowship of the Ring*

4. **Intoxicated with the heavens**, he couldn't imagine needing anything on earth.
   Katherine Paterson, *Bridge to Terabithia*

5. **When the child went to her room and was about to climb into bed**, she found tucked away under the coverlet her old crumpled straw hat.
   Johanna Spyri, *Heidi*

PRACTICE 1: MATCHING

Match the opener with its sentence. Write out each sentence, inserting the opener at the caret (^) and underlining it. Name the kind of opener—*word, phrase,* or *dependent clause*. There are two of each kind. **Punctuation:** Use a comma after an opener.

Sentences:

Openers:

1. ^, Nancy stood like a stone image, gazing down into the face of Jacob Aborn.

   Carolyn Keene, *Nancy Drew: The Bungalow Mystery*

   a. Taking the potion from the Wise Man

2. ^, none of the new spiders ever quite took Charlotte's place in his heart.

   E. B. White, *Charlotte's Web*

   b. When I turned around and the dog saw me coming

3. ^, pies were baking in the oven.

   Ray Bradbury, "I See You Never"

   c. Spellbound

4. ^, I turned on the light and caught my nightmare sitting at the foot of my bed.

   Mercer Mayer, "There's a Nightmare in My Closet"

   d. Although Wilbur the pig loved the spider's children and grandchildren dearly

5. ^, the young man drank it in a single gulp, and immediately fell into a deep sleep.

   Winifred Finlay, "The Water-Horse of Barra"

   e. Quickly

6. ^, he went off into the woods.

   Phyllis Reynolds Naylor, *Shiloh*

   f. Inside Mrs. O'Brien's kitchen

PRACTICE 2: DOWNSIZING

Boil it down. Get the skinny. Everybody wants the bottom line. Why? To save time. Combine each pair of sentences by making the bold part an opener for the other sentence. The result is the sentence the smart author wrote to begin with—just one sentence to say the same thing, but in a shorter way! Forget supersizing. Downsize instead: fewer calories, fewer words.

For better eating, get the skinny. For better writing, grab the opener and put it at the beginning of the sentence.

Don't forget the comma after the opener. It's naked without it.

EXAMPLE

Oversized: *(two sentences)*
Grandpa let out a yell. He was **throwing back his head**.

Downsized: *(one sentence with **opener**)*
Throwing back his head, Grandpa let out a yell.

Wilson Rawls, *Where the Red Fern Grows*

Words:

1. Eragon was **tired**. Eragon fell asleep with the small dragon cradled against him.

Christopher Paolini, *Eragon*

2. Ralph was **desperate**. Ralph climbed back into the ambulance.

Beverly Cleary, *The Mouse and the Motorcycle*

3. Taran heard a thrashing among the leaves. The sound came from **ahead**.

Lloyd Alexander, *The Book of Three*

4. The boy fastened the collar on the bear cub. He did it **reluctantly**.

Hal Borland, *When the Legends Die*

5. Charles Wallace buried his face in the unicorn's mane, with his fingers clenching the silver strands as the wind tried to drag him from the unicorn's back. Charles Wallace was **retching** during all of it.

Madeleine L'Engle, *A Swiftly Tilting Planet*

Phrases:

6. They were **on the big ship**. Things began to happen.

Hans Augusto Rey, *Curious George*

7. He was **grabbing his bloody nose in both hands**. He started rocking and moaning.

Wilson Rawls, *Where the Red Fern Grows*

8. Jemmy acted on instinct. He was **a thoroughbred of the streets**.

   Sid Fleischman, *The Whipping Boy*

9. Ramona scrubbed her face with her soggy Kleenex. Ramona had been **comforted by unexpected support from her sister**.

   Beverly Cleary, *Ramona the Brave*

10. He lowered his eyes. He did this **to hide his tears**.

    Bill and Vera Cleaver, *Where the Lilies Bloom*

Dependent Clauses:

11. Something happened **as she stepped forward**. The wharf tilted upward and she felt curiously lightheaded.

    Elizabeth George Speare, *The Witch of Blackbird Pond*

12. I built a fire. I built it **after the bed was made**.

    Wilson Rawls, *Where the Red Fern Grows*

13. The puppy licked his face raw and sent a stream down his jacket front. The puppy did those things **before Jess got to the creek bed**.

    Katherine Paterson, *Bridge to Terabithia*

14. There was much talk and excitement in Hobbiton. The talk and excitement happened **when Mr. Bilbo Baggins of Bag End announced that he would shortly be celebrating his eleventy-first birthday with a party of special magnificence**.

    J. R. R. Tolkien, *The Lord of the Rings: The Fellowship of the Ring*

15. Then the whole journey is pointless. It's pointless **if you have no intention of loving or being loved**.

    Kate DeCamillo, *The Miraculous Journey of Edward Tulane*

PRACTICE 3: UNSCRAMBLING TO IMITATE

Unscramble both lists of sentence parts to imitate the same model. Tell what part is an opener. Then write your own imitation of the model using something from your imagination, or from a TV show, movie, story, or book.

MODEL: In the morning, a short man came climbing through the trash and rubble.

Kate DiCamillo, *The Miraculous Journey of Edward Tulane*

List One:

a. sat playing with the toys and dolls

b. in her room

c. a small child

Imitation: In her room, a small child sat playing with the toys and dolls. *(phrase opener)*

List Two:

a. was removing the weeds and debris

b. at the garden

c. a strong man

Imitation: At the garden, a strong man was removing the weeds and debris. *(phrase opener)*

FIRST MODEL: Puzzled, Nancy and Helen climbed into the convertible, and Nancy started the engine.

Carolyn Keene, *Nancy Drew: The Bungalow Mystery*

1a. and Rhea pocketed the change

1b. Rhea and Roger

1c. irritated

1d. argued over the amount

2a. and Mike began the rescue

2b. Mike and Kevin

2c. horrified

2d. gazed into the flames

SECOND MODEL: Hungry, Thomas ate two portions of meat, nothing else.

Hal Borland, *When the Legends Die*

3a. only that

3b. wanted ten minutes of sleep

3c. tired

3d. Henry

4a. only two

4b. asked two questions about it

4c. curious

4d. Betsy

THIRD MODEL: Huffing slightly, he walked over to the boxing ring.

Robert Lipsyte, *The Contender*

5a. strolled over

5b. singing softly

5c. to the baby's crib

5d. the sitter

6a. ran over

6b. acting quickly

6c. to the accident victim

6d. the doctor

FOURTH MODEL: Undaunted by their failure to catch the thief, the Hardy boys left police headquarters with Chet Morton.

Franklin W. Dixon, *The Hardy Boys: The Tower Treasure*

7a. about their strategy

7b. the two girls

7c. discouraged by their inability to get the answer

7d. asked someone else

8a. with her voice coach

8b. the young soprano

8c. excited by the request to perform a solo

8d. practiced the song

FIFTH MODEL: When the people in Central Park learned that one of the toy sailboats was being steered by a mouse in a sailor suit, they all came running.

E. B. White, *Stuart Little*

9a. they all started whining

9b. was being delivered by the man in the ice cream truck

9c. that none of the expected ice cream

9d. after the children in nursery school heard

10a. they all stopped playing

10b. were being mistreated by an adult with an ugly tattoo

10c. that some of the teenage audience

10d. when the members of the band saw

PRACTICE 4: EXCHANGING

Sometimes you take something back to a store to exchange it. Although you can't take openers back to a store, you can still exchange them to practice writing good openers.

If the opener is a word, exchange it for a new word. If the opener is a phrase, get a new phrase. If the opener is a dependent clause, trade it in for a new dependent clause. Write out the complete sentence.

EXAMPLE: WORD OPENER

Original sentence: **Fortunately**, the door was not particularly sturdy and gave way easily.

Franklin W. Dixon, The Hardy Boys: The House on the Cliff

Sample Exchanges:

- **Rotted**, the door was not particularly sturdy and gave way easily.

- **Creaking**, the door was not particularly sturdy and gave way easily.

- **Luckily**, the door was not particularly sturdy and gave way easily.

---

1. **Surprised**, Troy craned his neck for a better look, but other students kept getting in the way.

   N. B. Grace, High School Musical: The Junior Novel

2. **Miserable**, he wandered about the many tents, only to find that one place was as cold as another.

   Jack London, The Call of the Wild

3. **Slowly**, she built up the nest until she was sitting on a big grassy mound.

   E. B. White, The Trumpet of the Swan

4. **Discouraged**, she wriggled backward down the frost heave and arrived at her camp feet first.

   Jean Craighead George, Julie of the Wolves

5. **Fading**, they sighed that sunlight and birds, bright mornings, warm fires, food and drink, friendship, and all good things had been lost beyond recovery.

   Lloyd Alexander, The Book of Three

EXAMPLE: PHRASE OPENER

Original sentence: **Creeping without sound through the underbrush**, he at last came to a thicket at the very edge of the water.

Elizabeth Coatsworth, "The Story of Wang Li"

Sample Exchanges:

- **Exhausted from being chased from his camp by the bear**, he at last came to a thicket at the very edge of the water.

- **Happy to end his hike through the woods,** he at last came to a thicket at the very edge of the water.

- **After searching all day in the woods for his lost dog,** he at last came to a thicket at the very edge of the water.

---

6. **Humming softly,** Nancy went to the modern pink-and-white kitchen.

   Carolyn Keene, *Nancy Drew: The Bungalow Mystery*

7. **At the crossroads over the bridge,** he met two friends, and the three of them walked to school together, making ridiculous strides and being rather silly.

   John Steinbeck, *The Red Pony*

8. **To qualify for the racing team in junior high,** she would have to practice every day.

   Eleanor Coerr, *Sadako and the Thousand Paper Cranes*

9. **Quick as a flash,** the boy leaped forward and grabbed the ball from Charles Wallace's hand, then darted back into the shadows.

   Madeleine L'Engle, *A Wrinkle in Time*

10. **Pursued by killer whales,** the bass fish had tried to escape by swimming toward shore.

    Joseph Krumgold, *Onion John*

EXAMPLE: DEPENDENT CLAUSE OPENER

Original sentence: **When I left my office that beautiful spring day,** I had no idea what was in store for me.

   Wilson Rawls, *Where the Red Fern Grows*

Sample Exchanges:

- **When Ms. Wanker told me to go to the principal's office because I wouldn't stop pulling Peggy's ponytail,** I had no idea what was in store for me.

- **Since I had been knocked unconscious from the fall and taken to the emergency room,** I had no idea what was in store for me.

- **Although everybody else knew what to expect,** I had no idea what was in store for me.

11. **After a rock hit Billy over the eye**, he sat down backward in the mud, covering his head with his arms, sobbing.

    Thomas Rockwell, *How to Eat Fried Worms*

12. **As the prisoners were carried up to the ambulance with the others following**, Lieutenant Gill explained to the Dowds how Nancy had saved them from being burned in the wreckage.

    Carolyn Keene, *Nancy Drew: The Bungalow Mystery*

13. **Although the Hardy boys felt that it would be a useless search**, they agreed to go along.

    Franklin W. Dixon, *The Hardy Boys: The Tower Treasure*

14. **Before I emerged**, I made certain my mask was securely tied.

    Gail Carson Levine, *Ella Enchanted*

15. **When the boy came home after each long trip in search of his father**, the crippled hound dog would hobble far down the road to meet him, wag his tail, stand on his hind legs, and paw the boy with his good front paw.

    William H. Armstrong, *Sounder*

PRACTICE 5: IMITATING SENTENCES BY AUTHORS

Match the imitation with its model sentence. Then write your own imitation of the model using something from your imagination, or from a TV show, movie, story, or book. Cheers to you for writing like an author.

Model Sentences:

1. Because she was wearing his jeans and his shirt, it was like looking into a fun-house mirror.

    Kate DiCamillo, *The Tiger Rising*

2. Excitedly, the brothers speculated on the possible meaning of this clue.

    Franklin W. Dixon, *The Hardy Boys: The Secret of the Old Mill*

3. Flapping his wings as hard as he could from a thousand feet above the ocean, the seagull pushed over into a blazing steep dive toward the waves.

    Richard Bach, *Jonathan Livingston Seagull*

4. Holding a hand before her eyes so that other patients and visitors should not see, she began to weep.

J. M. Coetzee, *Life and Times of Michael K*

5. When Mr. Berman waits on us, buying shoes is almost fun.

Judy Blume, *Tales of a Fourth Grade Nothing*

Imitations:

A. Instinctively, the dog sniffed out the only bone in the yard.

B. Moving his legs as fast as he could in a marathon race around the city, James hung on for a respectable fast finish at the end.

C. Keeping a dollar in her pocket so that unexpected circumstances and opportunities could not escape, she started to travel.

D. As the sun sets over the ocean, looking out is always beautiful.

E. Since she was remembering her unhappiness and her tears, it was like moving into a dark closet.

PRACTICE 6: EXPANDING

There's more than one way to comb your hair, arrange your room, wash your dog, or tease your little brother or sister. There's more than one way to open a sentence. For each sentence add a *word*, then a *phrase*, then a *dependent clause*.

EXAMPLE

[OPENER GOES HERE], she noticed very soon one little girl, about her own age, who looked at her very hard with a pair of light, rather dull, blue eyes.

Word: **Staring**, she noticed very soon one little girl, about her own age, who looked at her very hard with a pair of light, rather dull, blue eyes.

Phrase: **Near the edge of the playground after school**, she noticed very soon one little girl, about her own age, who looked at her very hard with a pair of light, rather dull, blue eyes.

Dependent clause: **After Gabriella entered the theater to see the play about the little mermaid**, she noticed very soon one little girl, about her own age, who looked at her very hard with a pair of light, rather dull, blue eyes.

Original sentence: **When Sara sat at Miss Munchkin's side,** she noticed very soon one little girl, about her own age, who looked at her very hard with a pair of light, rather dull, blue eyes.

Frances Hodgson Burnett, *A Little Princess*

---

1. ^, Harriet left the dining room.

   Louise Fitzhugh, *Harriet the Spy*

2. ^, he clapped his hands and laughed.

   Judy Blume, *Tales of a Fourth Grade Nothing*

3. ^, she had an almost overwhelming desire to look around, to see what was behind the other doors and down the other corridors.

   Robert C. O'Brien, *Mrs. Frisby and the Rats of NIMH*

4. ^, Sophie caught a glimpse of an enormous long pale wrinkly face with the most enormous ears.

   Roald Dahl, *The BFG*

5. ^, he had been badly sun-burned during the day, and he kept twisting and turning on the raft in a vain attempt to find a comfortable position.

   Arthur C. Clarke, *Dolphin Island*

STORY GRAMMAR

Using one of the authors' sentences as a starter sentence, write the opening paragraph of a story. The complete story will take lots of pages to tell, but your job is to write just the first paragraph, at least five sentences long. Write your sentences so well that the author of your starter sentence would say, "Great job!"

- Just as the authors' sentences use openers, within your paragraph use *openers and other sentence-composing tools to make your paragraph sparkle and shine.* For your openers, use at least one word, one phrase, one dependent clause as tools.

- Exchange your rough draft with drafts of other students in your class to get suggestions for improvement. Use suggestions to revise your paragraph to make it better.

■ Publish your writing by reading your paragraph to the class or posting it online. See how other students who used your same starter sentence wrote their first paragraphs to begin that long story.

Openers Are **Bold:**

1. **After he came to himself,** he was lying in a firelit place with bruised limbs and a bad headache.

   C. S. Lewis, *The Chronicles of Narnia: Prince Caspian*

2. **Leaving her backpack, leaving the plastic bag of groceries,** Lucky ran down the road to find her dog.

   Susan Patron, *The Higher Power of Lucky*

3. **Inside,** the restaurant was warm and bright and smelled like fried chicken and toast and coffee.

   Kate DiCamillo, *The Miraculous Journey of Edward Tulane*

4. **At three o'clock,** the school bus pulled up, belching and gasping and sighing.

   Kate DiCamillo, *The Tiger Rising*

5. **When he found seven hundred and twenty-one and one-half dead lab rats in his locker, packed in tightly,** the flies stayed for a month even when the rats were gone.

   Gary Paulsen, *The Time Hackers*

Tip for Better Revising: Always, when you revise something you've written, look for places to use openers plus other sentence-composing tools to add detail and dazzle to your writing.

Review: An opener is a word, phrase, or dependent clause that begins a sentence.

Preview: You'll learn another good position to put words, phrases, or dependent clauses. This one has a funny name: *S-V split.* (Are you laughing yet?)

S-V Split

Do you have an older and younger brother or sister? If so, you're in the middle, a good place to be because you get help from the older one and give help to the younger one. Good things often happen in the middle (including middle school).

Same thing happens with sentences. Authors sometimes put details in the middle of a sentence, between the subject and its verb, because the information works best there. Take a look at sentences without a tool in the middle, and then compare them to sentences with a tool in the middle called an *S-V split* because it splits a subject from its verb:

1. The August sun was warm on our bare heads.

2. The twins were allowed to watch half an hour of TV.

3. The giant peach was like a massive golden ball sailing upon a silver sea.

4. The meat hung in the smoke-house.

5. One of the rocks jutted out of the water almost at the boat's side.

There's not much detail or dazzle in those sentences. Now look at how the authors actually wrote their sentences, this time with *S-V splits*:

1. The August sun, **full now in mid-morning**, was warm on our bare heads.
   Bill and Vera Cleaver, *Where the Lilies Bloom*

2. The twins, **who had finished their homework**, were allowed to watch half an hour of TV.
   Madeleine L'Engle, *A Wrinkle in Time*

3. The giant peach, **with the sunlight glinting on its side**, was like a massive golden ball sailing upon a silver sea.
   Roald Dahl, *James and the Giant Peach*

4. The meat, **dry-cured for the feeding of the dogs**, hung in the smoke-house.
   Marjorie Kinnan Rawlings, *The Yearling*

5. One of the rocks, **black and sharp like an ugly tooth**, jutted out of the water almost at the boat's side.

> Franklin W. Dixon, *The Hardy Boys: The House on the Cliff*

PRACTICE 1: MATCHING

Match the S-V split with its sentence. Write out each sentence, inserting the S-V split at the caret (^) and underlining it. Name the kind of S-V split—*word, phrase,* or *dependent clause*. There are two of each kind. **Punctuation:** Use commas before and after an S-V split.

Sentences:

1. An elderly woman, ^, stepped out.

> Mildred D. Taylor, *Roll of Thunder, Hear My Cry*

2. The women, ^, now must take the place of the men and face the dangers beyond the village.

> Scott O'Dell, *Island of the Blue Dolphins*

3. Chantilly, ^, was sunning on the porch steps.

> Patricia C. McKissack, "A Million Fish, More or Less"

4. Gwydion, ^, sat with his knees drawn up and his back against an enormous elm.

> Alexander Lloyd, *The Book of Three*

5. Gilly, ^, went back to school.

> Katherine Paterson, *The Great Gilly Hopkins*

6. The first floor, ^, was where the rats lived.

> Walter Dean Myers, *Motown and Didi*

S-V Splits:

a. because it was closest to the garbage in the empty lot

b. watchful

c. armed with an absence excuse more like a commendation for bravery in battle

d. toothless

e. who were never asked to do more than stay at home, cook food, and make clothing

f. the neighbor girl's cat

PRACTICE 2: DOWNSIZING

Boil it down. Get the skinny. Everybody wants the bottom line. Why? To save time. Combine each pair of sentences by making the bold part an *S-V split* for the other sentence. The result is the sentence the smart author wrote to begin with— just one sentence to say the same thing, but in a shorter way! Forget supersizing. Downsize instead: fewer calories, fewer words.

For better eating, get the skinny. For better writing, grab the S-V split and put it between the subject and its verb.

Don't forget the commas before and after the S-V split. It's naked without them.

EXAMPLE

Oversized: *(two sentences)*
Ramona's feet ^ carried her slowly towards home. They were **no longer light with joy**.

Downsized: *(one sentence with S-V split)*
Ramona's feet, **no longer light with joy**, carried her slowly towards home.

Beverly Cleary, *Ramona the Pest*

Words:

1. The horse ^ reared slightly. The horse was **startled**.

Lynne Reid Banks, *The Indian in the Cupboard*

2. Sophie ^ saw several tremendous tall figures moving among the rocks about five hundred yards away. She was **squinting**.

Roald Dahl, *The BFG*

3. At one point a raven ^ flapped out from a bush and flew alongside us. The raven was **lustrous**.

Bill and Vera Cleaver, *Where the Lilies Bloom*

4. The china rabbit's head ^ had been in twenty-one pieces and now was put back together into one. This was **apparently** so.

Kate DiCamillo, *The Miraculous Journey of Edward Tulane*

5. A trail of blood ^ followed him. It was **smeared**.

William H. Armstrong, *Sounder*

Phrases:

6. Henry ^ is always making jokes about me and Sheila. Henry is **the elevator operator**.

   Judy Blume, *Tales of a Fourth Grade Nothing*

7. Her father's voice ^ sounded hollow and far away. His voice was **coming through the furnace pipes**.

   Beverly Cleary, *Ramona and Her Father*

8. The fish ^ was frying in the pan. The fish was **covered with onions**.

   Louis Sachar, *There's a Boy in the Girls' Bathroom*

9. The Monster ^ lunged forward with a terrible scream. It lunged forward **at the first motion**.

   Ray Bradbury, "A Sound of Thunder"

10. The first student ^ took the stage. The student was **a shy boy with a slightly flat voice**.

    N. B. Grace, *High School Musical: The Junior Novel*

Dependent Clauses:

11. Lesley ^ abandoned her half of the wide handle and leaped out of the way. Leslie abandoned it **when she felt the lawn mower bearing down on her**.

    Lynne Reid Banks, *One More River*

12. Gwydion ^ caught sight of them instantly. Gwydion was the one **whose eyes were everywhere at once**.

    Lloyd Alexander, *The Book of Three*

13. Mrs. Rachel ^ took mental note of everything that was on that table. She did this **before she closed the door**.

    L. M. Montgomery, *Anne of Green Gables*

14. Mr. Posey ^ told the truth. Mr. Posey was the one **who was close to tears by now**.

    Jean Merrill, *The Pushcart War*

15. The aspirin pill ^ came up again promptly, along with the bowl of soup she'd coaxed down earlier. It was the pill **which she got down the boy's throat with no little difficulty**.

> Katherine Paterson, *The Great Gilly Hopkins*

PRACTICE 3: UNSCRAMBLING TO IMITATE

Unscramble both lists of sentence parts to imitate the same model. Tell what part is an S-V split. Then write your own imitation of the model using something from your imagination, or from a TV show, movie, story, or book.

EXAMPLE

MODEL: One heavyweight, a loud guy whose handlers all wore black silk jackets, brought along his own disk jockey.

> Robert Lipsyte, *The Brave*

List One:

a. a charming woman whose students all spoke perfect, fluent French

b. talked about her own native experience

c. one teacher

Imitation: One teacher, a charming woman whose students all spoke perfect, fluent French, talked about her own native experience.

List Two:

a. a small man whose teammates all wore bright silk shirts

b. brought along his own cheering squad

c. one bowler

Imitation: One bowler, a small man whose teammates all wore bright silk shirts, brought along his own cheering squad.

FIRST MODEL: Uncle Hammer, leaning against the fireplace mantel, did not laugh.

> Mildred D. Taylor, *Roll of Thunder, Hear My Cry*

1a. did not stop

1b. opening up the birthday gift

1c. Susie Stockton

2a. did not yell

2b. watching over the young children

2c. Buddy Brown

SECOND MODEL: Patrice Wilkins, who sat in front of Rob in class, snorted and then giggled and then covered her mouth.

Kate DiCamillo, *The Tiger Rising*

3a. who looked out over the playing fields on campus

3b. Chris Burke

3c. then treasured the memories

3d. smiled and then remembered and

4a. who stood in front of the congregation each week

4b. the clergyman

4c. then delivered his sermon

4d. prayed and then sang and

THIRD MODEL: Ben, the youngest brother, was licking a black crayon and marking prices on soap-flake boxes when they walked in.

Robert Lipsyte, *The Contender*

5a. while others jumped around

5b. Jefferson

5c. was nibbling a treat and wagging his tail in the puppy pen

5d. the smallest puppy

6a. after the store opened up

6b. Kira

6c. was holding a snowball and getting money from her purse

6d. the first customer

FOURTH MODEL: The dog, whose rhythmic panting came through the porch floor, came from under the house and began to whine.

William H. Armstrong, *Sounder*

7a. and began to purr

7b. whose fluffy fur spilled over the velvet sofa

7c. came from under the pillow

7d. the cat

8a. and began to laugh

8b. whose wobbly feet stumbled over everything

8c. persisted with a big grin

8d. the toddler

FIFTH MODEL: The horses, listening, pricked up their ears when they heard the goose hollering.

E. B. White, *Charlotte's Web*

9a. the dolls	10a. the gardeners
9b. after they saw the children entering	10b. while they watched the rabbits playing
9c. put on their smiles	10c. held up their digging
9d. hoping	10d. resting

PRACTICE 4: EXCHANGING

Sometimes you take something back to a store to exchange it. Although you can't take S-V splits back to a store, you can still exchange them to practice writing good S-V splits.

If the S-V split is a *word*, exchange it for a new word. If the S-V split is a *phrase*, get a new phrase. If the S-V split is a *dependent clause*, trade it in for a new dependent clause. Write out the complete sentence.

EXAMPLE: WORD S-V SPLIT

Original sentence: The four children, **panting**, found themselves standing in a woody place.

C. S. Lewis, *The Chronicles of Narnia: Prince Caspian*

Sample Exchanges:

- The four children, **afraid**, found themselves standing in a woody place.
- The four children, **finally**, found themselves standing in a woody place.
- The four children, **wandering**, found themselves standing in a woody place.

1. The curtains, **red**, with a blue and green geometrical pattern, were drawn, and seemed to reflect their cheerfulness throughout the room.

Madeleine L'Engle, *A Wrinkle in Time*

2. A woman of fifty or so, **plump**, with frizzy gray hair, came toward them down the dark hall.

Katherine Paterson, *Park's Quest*

3. A shaft of sunlight, **warm**, lay across his body.

   Marjorie Kinnan Rawling, *The Yearling*

4. A circle of grass, **smooth**, met her eyes, with dark trees dancing all round it.

   C. S. Lewis, *The Chronicles of Narnia: Prince Caspian*

5. Neither boy had on shoes, and their Sunday clothing, **patched**, hung loosely upon their frail frames. *(Two sentences connected by a comma plus* and. *The S-V split is in the second sentence.)*

   Mildred D. Taylor, *Roll of Thunder, Hear My Cry*

EXAMPLE: PHRASE S-V SPLIT ———————————————————

Original sentence: Zeke, **one of the basketball players**, watched Sharpay as she haughtily pushed her way through the crowd.

   N. B. Grace, *High School Musical: The Junior Novel*

Sample Exchanges:

■ Zeke, **to get her attention and maybe a date**, watched Sharpay as she haughtily pushed her way through the crowd.

■ Zeke, **standing near the bus stop after the concert**, watched Sharpay as she haughtily pushed her way through the crowd.

■ Zeke, **my older brother with a crush on her**, watched Sharpay as she haughtily pushed her way through the crowd.

6. He, **at fourteen**, was pudgy, bespectacled, and totally unsentimental.

   Katherine Paterson, *Jacob Have I Loved*

7. A child's voice, **coming from behind a nearby bush**, made the sound.

   Lois Lowry, *The Giver*

8. Only Frith, **the goose girl**, feared him not at all.

   Elinor Mordaunt, "The Prince and the Goose Girl"

9. The canoe, **stripped of sail and mast**, twisted and shifted in the rushing waters.

   Armstrong Sperry, *Call It Courage*

10. Curtis and Doug, **two of Jeff's friends**, came out of Mrs. Sharp's class.

Louis Sachar, *There's a Boy in the Girls' Bathroom*

EXAMPLE: DEPENDENT CLAUSE S-V SPLIT ———————————

Original sentence: Mr. Quimby, **who had a dish towel tucked into his belt for an apron**, turned from the kitchen sink.

Beverly Cleary, *Ramona and Her Father*

Sample Exchanges:

■ Mr. Quimby, **whose wife called him from the living room**, turned from the kitchen sink.

■ Mr. Quimby, **because the faucet burst and was spraying him with water**, turned from the kitchen sink.

■ Mr. Quimby, **after he did the dishes from supper**, turned from the kitchen sink.

11. Mr. McAlester, **who owned the store**, was a good Arkansas man.

Charles Portis, *True Grit*

12. The truck drivers, **when they heard that Maxie Hammerman had been released**, were furious.

Jean Merrill, *The Pushcart War*

13. The old woman beside him, **whose arm he held**, was hunched over as she shuffled along in her soft slippers.

Lois Lowry, *The Giver*

14. Nellie, **before she put him to bed each night**, sang Edward a lullaby, a song about a mockingbird that did not sing and a diamond ring that would not shine.

Kate DiCamillo, *The Miraculous Journey of Edward Tulane*

15. The Badger, **who wore a long dressing-gown**, and **whose slippers were indeed very down-at-heel**, carried a candlestick in his paw. *(Contains two S-V splits.)*

Kenneth Grahame, *The Wind in the Willows*

PRACTICE 5: IMITATING SENTENCES BY AUTHORS

Match the imitation with its model sentence. Then write your own imitation of the model about something using your imagination, or from a TV show, movie, story, or book. Cheers to you for writing like an author.

Model Sentences:

1. Carson Drew, startled, looked at his daughter.

> Carolyn Keene, *Nancy Drew: The Bungalow Mystery*

2. Heidi, who had never seen so huge a cat, stopped to admire it.

> Johanna Spyri, *Heidi*

3. Over the countryside, neighbors, leaning against slanting porch posts and standing in open cabin doorways, knew that it was the dog. *(Contains two S-V splits.)*

> William H. Armstrong, *Sounder*

4. The bull's flanks were wet, and his weapons, the horns, were curved and ended in a needle of danger. *(Two sentences connected by a comma plus* and. *The S-V split is in the second sentence.)*

> Maia Wojciechowska, *Shadow of a Bull*

5. Then the villagers, houseless and foodless, fled down the valley, and their village, shredded and tossed and trampled, melted behind them. *(Two sentences connected by a comma plus* and. *S-V splits are in both sentences.)*

> Rudyard Kipling, *The Jungle Book*

Imitations:

A. Before the thunder clap, the audience, looking up at the dark sky and waiting on the unprotected grass, hoped that it was acceptable weather.

B. The child's playtime was wonderful, and his toys, his entertainment, were fun and contained in a room of happiness.

C. John Crocker, amused, listened to his son-in-law.

D. Virginia, who had always made the best applesauce, started to taste it.

E. Now the birds, loud and frantic, flew through the trees, and the sky, angry and violent and stormy, raged around them.

PRACTICE 6: EXPANDING

There's more than one way to comb your hair, arrange your room, wash your dog, or tease your little brother or sister. There's more than one way to use an S-V split in a sentence. For each sentence add a *word*, then a *phrase*, then a *dependent clause*.

EXAMPLE

Jody, [S-V SPLIT GOES HERE], straightened up as the ranch hand sauntered out of the barn.

Word: Jody, **worried**, straightened up as the ranch hand sauntered out of the barn.

Phrase: Jody, **the cousin visiting the farm from the city**, straightened up as the ranch hand sauntered out of the barn.

Dependent clause: Jody, **who didn't want to be caught teasing the pigs**, straightened up as the ranch hand sauntered out of the barn.

Original sentence: Jody, **who was helping Doubletree Mutt**, straightened up as the ranch hand sauntered out of the barn. *(dependent clause)*

John Steinbeck, *The Red Pony*

---

1. Nancy, ^, grinned up at her friend.

    Carolyn Keene, *Nancy Drew: The Mystery at Lilac Inn*

2. Both Hardy boys, ^, decided to stay and see what they could find out.

    Franklin W. Dixon, *The Hardy Boys: The Secret of the Old Mill*

3. The gwythaints, ^, grew larger and larger as they plunged toward horse and riders.

    Lloyd Alexander, *The Book of Three*

4. A woman, ^, stood before them.

    Harry Allard, *Miss Nelson Is Missing!*

5. This leader, ^, was no more than twelve or thirteen years old and looked even younger.

    Henry Gregor Felsen, "Horatio"

STORY GRAMMAR

Using one of the authors' sentences as a starter sentence, write the opening paragraph of a story. The complete story will take lots of pages to tell, but your job is to write just the first paragraph, at least five sentences long. Write your sentences so well that the author of your starter sentence would say, "Great job!"

- Just as the authors' sentences use S-V splits, within your paragraph use *S-V splits and other sentence-composing tools to make your paragraph sparkle and shine.* For your S-V splits, use at least one word, one phrase, and one dependent clause as tools.

- Exchange your rough draft with drafts of other students in your class to get suggestions for improvement. Use suggestions to revise your paragraph to make it better.

- Publish your writing by reading your paragraph to the class or posting it online. See how other students who used your same starter sentence wrote their first paragraphs to begin that long story.

S-V Splits Are **Bold:**

1. Marcel the dog, **looking out from the shadows of the alley**, began to bark.

   Chris Van Allsburg, *The Sweetest Fig*

2. His laptop, **which was rolled up in his back pocket**, was insistently signaling that he had an urgent message.

   Gary Paulsen, *The Time Hackers*

3. In the meadow, early one morning, Petunia, **the silly goose**, went strolling.

   Roger Duvoisin, "Petunia"

4. The curtains, **moving in the breeze**, were like the sea's foam.

   William H. Armstrong, *Sounder*

5. The man, **dressed all in white, riding a milk-white horse**, galloped swiftly around the corner of the hut, leaped the wall, and disappeared.

   Post Wheeler, "Vasilissa the Beautiful"

Tip for Better Revising: Always, when you revise something you've written, look for places to use S-V splits plus other sentence-composing tools to add detail and dazzle to your writing.

Review: An S-V split is a word, phrase, or dependent clause that comes between a subject and its verb.

Preview: Now you'll learn another good position to put words, phrases, or dependent clauses. You've learned about openers and S-V splits, so what's the next position? What's the only position left? To see if you're right, turn the page.

Closer

Some things are better last, at the end (especially happy endings). What part of a meal is at the end? It's dessert, of course. Good things come to those who wait.

In their sentences, sometimes authors make readers wait, putting information at the end because it's more useful there. Take a look at sentences without a tool at the end, and then better sentences with a tool saved for the end called a *closer* because it comes at the closing of a sentence:

1. Toby devoured long books not liked by his brother Pete.

2. The fly in the spider web was beating its wings furiously.

3. I sat down with my coffee and wished I had a medical book in the house.

4. I stared down at the animal skeleton.

5. On her way back she met the Prince.

There's not much detail or dazzle in those sentences. Now look at how the authors actually wrote their sentences, this time with *closers*:

1. Toby devoured long books not liked by his brother Pete, **whose reading is limited to a series of truly gross horror novels called *Fleshcrawlers*.**
   James Howe, *Bunnicula Strikes Again!*

2. The fly in the spider web was beating its wings furiously, **trying to break loose and free itself.**
   E. B. White, *Charlotte's Web*

3. I sat down with my coffee and wished I had a medical book in the house, **something that might give me some clues on how to help him.**
   Cynthia Rylant, *Missing May*

4. I stared down at the animal skeleton, **lying so clean and perfect on the ground.**
   R. L. Stine, *Ghost Beach*

5. On her way back she met the Prince, **who pulled up his horse and scowled at her so that she might not see the love in his eyes.**

Elinor Mordaunt, "The Prince and the Goose Girl"

PRACTICE 1: MATCHING

Match the closer with its sentence. Write out each sentence, inserting the closer at the caret (^) and underlining it. Name the kind of closer—*word*, *phrase*, or *dependent clause*. There are two of each kind.

Sentences:

1. There was Crook Arm, ^.

   Laurence Yep, *Dragonwings*

2. She set two fried eggs before him with two slabs of coarse bread, ^.

   William Barrett, *The Lilies of the Field*

3. Gilly gave little William Ernest the most fearful face in all her repertory of scary looks, ^.

   Katherine Paterson, *The Great Gilly Hopkins*

4. I started calling him Fang ^.

   Judy Blume, *Tales of a Fourth Grade Nothing*

5. In the fishpond, the hippo belched, ^.

   Leon Hugo, "My Father and the Hippopotamus"

6. Then Jesse gave a great whoop and leapt into the stream, ^.

   Natalie Babbitt, *Tuck Everlasting*

Closers:

a. because when he smiles all you can see are the top two side teeth next to the big space

b. not softly

c. sort of a cross between Count Dracula and Godzilla

d. toasted

e. splashing mightily

f. whose left arm dangled down uselessly by his side with two of his fingers missing

PRACTICE 2: DOWNSIZING

Boil it down. Get the skinny. Everybody wants the bottom line. Why? To save time. Combine each pair of sentences by making the bold part a closer for the other sentence. The result is the sentence the smart author wrote to begin with—just one sentence to say the same thing, but in a shorter way! Forget supersizing. Downsize instead: fewer calories, fewer words.

For better eating, get the skinny. For better writing, grab the closer and put it at the end of the sentence.

Don't forget the comma before the closer. It's naked without it.

EXAMPLE

Oversized: *(two sentences)*
School seemed a million miles away. It was as if it were **a moon that she had been to once.**

Downsized: *(one sentence with closer)*
School seemed a million miles away, **a moon that she had been to once.**

Louise Fitzhugh, *Harriet the Spy*

Words:

1. The huge boiled night crawler worm sprawled limply in the center of the platter. The worm was **steaming**.

   Thomas Rockwell, *How to Eat Fried Worms*

2. Gwydion sat upright. He was **tense**.

   Lloyd Alexander, *The Book of Three*

3. The man was about fifty. He was **overweight**.

   Frank Bonham, *Chief*

4. As the bull reached the cape, the man swung it alongside. He swung it **slowly**.

   Maia Wojciechowska, *Shadow of a Bull*

5. His hair was almost gold in color. It was **gleaming**.

   John Christopher, *The Guardians*

Phrases:

6. On and on ran Ralph the mouse. He ran **down the hill, under doors, around and under beds and dressers.**

   Beverly Cleary, *The Mouse and the Motorcycle*

7. He was carrying a book. It was **my old worn-out picture dictionary**.

   Judy Blume, *Tales of a Fourth Grade Nothing*

8. He must be up early in the morning. He had **to milk the cow and bring in wood and work the crops.**

   Marjorie Kinnan Rawlings, *The Yearling*

9. They were all creatures of the wild. They were **accustomed to being hunted.**

   C. S. Lewis, *The Chronicles of Narnia: Prince Caspian*

10. The giant roared strange words at Tarik. They were **fearful words that made his skin crawl.**

    Walter Dean Myers, *Legend of Tarik*

Dependent Clauses:

11. Every girl in the seventh grade slides to the ground. This happens **when Willard Hughes walks by**. *(The closer needs no comma because there is no pause before it.)*

    Katherine Paterson, *Bridge to Terabithia*

12. They took the kitten into the house. Inside the house was **where the very old woman gave it a warm bath and brushed its fur until it was soft and shiny.**

    Wanda Gag, "Millions of Cats"

13. My heart was pounding. It was pounding **as Chester the cat unlocked the rabbit's cage door with his paw**. *(The closer needs no comma because there is no pause before it.)*

    Deborah and James Howe, *Bunnicula: A Rabbit-Tale of Mystery*

14. Vasilissa put the skull on the end of a stick and darted away through the forest, running as fast as she could and finding her path by the skull's glowing eyes. They were eyes **which went out only when morning came**.

Post Wheeler, "Vasilissa the Beautiful"

15. His arm grew numb, then began to prickle. He felt **as if hundreds of red-hot needles were jabbing him**.

Marguerite Henry, *Misty of Chincoteague*

PRACTICE 3: UNSCRAMBLING TO IMITATE

Unscramble both lists of sentence parts to imitate the same model. Tell what part is a closer. Then write your own imitation of the model using something from your imagination, or from a TV show, movie, story, or book.

EXAMPLE

MODEL: Sounder was making an awful noise, a strangled mixture of growl and bark.

William H. Armstrong, *Sounder*

List One:

a. a colorful rendering of fruit and flowers

b. was drawing an abstract painting

c. Liam

Imitation: Liam was drawing an abstract painting, a colorful rendering of fruit and flowers.

List Two:

a. an inherited recipe of hamburger and vegetables

b. was baking a tasty casserole

c. Geraldine

Imitation: Geraldine was baking a tasty casserole, an inherited recipe of hamburger and vegetables.

FIRST MODEL: Toad was in bed, taking a nap.

Arnold Lobel, *Frog and Toad Are Friends*

1a. was on the beach

1b. Maura Kate

1c. collecting some seashells

2a. was in art class

2b. Sam

2c. creating a statue

SECOND MODEL: I stood there before the whole court, crying.

Gail Carson Levine, *Ella Enchanted*

3a. smiling

3b. played then for the entire class

3c. the pianist

4a. pouring

4b. came here with a sudden arrival

4c. the rain

THIRD MODEL: The weary Mole had his head on his pillow, in great joy and contentment.

Kenneth Grahame, *The Wind in the Willows*

5a. had her hands on the book

5b. with great anticipation and excitement

5c. the eager girl

6a. hit the coast of the bay

6b. with great speed and damage

6c. the powerful hurricane

FOURTH MODEL: Ramona ran after Susan, whose curls bobbed daintily about her shoulder.

Beverly Cleary, *Ramona the Pest*

7a. whose arms extended reassuringly toward his daughter

7b. waddled toward her dad

7c. the toddler

8a. whose Frisbee dangled teasingly from his hand

8b. chased after its owner

8c. the dog

FIFTH MODEL: Wilbur planned to talk with Templeton, the rat from under his trough.

E. B. White, *Charlotte's Web*

9a. the band for sporting events

9b. wanted to play in Cymbals

9c. Brooks

10a. the girl with the latest moves

10b. tried to dance with Mandy

10c. Freddy

PRACTICE 4: EXCHANGING

Sometimes you take something back to a store to exchange it. Although you can't take closers back to a store, you can still exchange them to practice writing good closers.

If the closer is a *word*, exchange it for a new word. If the closer is a *phrase*, get a new phrase. If the closer is a *dependent clause*, trade it in for a new dependent clause. Write out the complete sentence.

EXAMPLE: WORD CLOSER

Original sentence: As the boy and his sister reached the beach, they turned back and watched, **breathless**.

Marguerite Henry, *Misty of Chincoteague*

Sample Exchanges:

- As the boy and his sister reached the beach, they turned back and watched, **waiting**.

- As the boy and his sister reached the beach, they turned back and watched, **excitedly**.

- As the boy and his sister reached the beach, they turned back and watched, **afraid**.

---

1. She wore old-fashioned glasses as she sat in an armchair, **knitting**.

Larry Weinberg, *Ghost Hotel*

2. The dragon in the iron cage was beautiful in his tiny ferocity and seemed happiest when flaming, his ruby eyes gleaming, **evilly**.

Gail Carson Levine, *Ella Enchanted*

3. Nobody said a word, **waiting**.

Cynthia Rylant, *Missing May*

4. Fulcher let Leslie run in the race, **grudgingly**.

Katherine Paterson, *Bridge to Terabithia*

5. The lion came bounding over, sniffed the rock a hundred times, walked around and around it, and went away, **puzzled**.

William Steig, "Sylvester and the Magic Pebble"

EXAMPLE: PHRASE CLOSER ————————————

Original sentence: Caleb and I looked at each other and burst out laughing remembering Hilly, **our old housekeeper.**

Patricia MacLachland, *Sarah, Plain and Tall*

Sample Exchanges:

- Caleb and I looked at each other and burst out laughing remembering Hilly, **for her silly magic tricks.**

- Caleb and I looked at each other and burst out laughing remembering Hilly, **with her pet worms in little boxes with straw.**

- Caleb and I looked at each other and burst out laughing remembering Hilly, **the girl with a big bump on her nose.**

6. Wilbur planned to have a talk with Templeton, **the rat that lived under his trough.**

E. B. White, *Charlotte's Web*

7. He had come west to rest, **to start over.**

Hal Borland, *When the Legends Die*

8. What attracted Mrs. Frisby's attention the most was a box in one corner of the room, **a box with dials and a small light shining on the front.**

Robert C. O'Brien, *Mrs. Frisby and the Rats of NIMH*

9. The dog made it safely to the bank and ran back, **shaking great drops of cold water on Jess.**

Katherine Paterson, *Bridge to Terabithia*

10. The pebble was flaming red, shiny, and perfectly round, **like a marble.**

William Steig, "Sylvester and the Magic Pebble"

DEPENDENT CLAUSE CLOSER ————————————

Original sentence: Rob was late for his English class **because he had to walk from the gym all the way to the front of the school.**

Kate DiCamillo, *The Tiger Rising*

Sample Exchanges:

- Rob was late for his English class **if he took too long after gym class to talk to his buddies.**

- Rob was late for his English class **because he went back to see if he had left his books in his last class.**

- Rob was late for his English class **when he stayed after class to talk to his math teacher about making up a quiz.**

NOTE: Sentences 11, 12, and 13 don't need a comma for the closer because there's no pause before their closers. Sentences 14 and 15 have a pause, so a comma is needed.

11. The old man looked up **when Jonas entered the room.**

    Lois Lowry, *The Giver*

12. He cried out in terror and hid his face **as the gwythaints veered off and swooped down.**

    Lloyd Alexander, *The Book of Three*

13. The first time the pony wore the bridle he whipped his head about and worked his tongue against the bit **until the blood oozed from the corners of his mouth.**

    John Steinbeck, *The Red Pony*

14. Sara opened the paper bag and took out one of the hot buns, **which had already warmed her own cold hands a little.**

    Frances Hodgson Burnett, *A Little Princess*

15. Birds flew to the tree-tops and seized the dwarves, **who were scrambling up now as far as they ever dared to go.**

    J. R. R. Tolkien, *The Hobbit*

PRACTICE 5: IMITATING AUTHORS

Match the imitation with its model sentence. Then write your own imitation of the model using something from your imagination, or from a TV show, movie, story, or book. Cheers to you for writing like an author.

Model Sentences:

1. Nobody was around but Snowball, the white cat belonging to Mrs. Little.

   E. B. White, *Stuart Little*

2. The superintendent checked the cellar storage cages after a passing youth hinted to him that there had been a robbery.

   Emily Neville, *It's Like This, Cat*

3. Numbly, Alfred lowered himself to the edge of one chair, clutching his shirt in his hands.

   Robert Lipsyte, *The Contender*

4. Behind her in the shadows, he could see the little boy, who was about his own age.

   Madeleine L'Engle, *A Wrinkle in Time*

5. Benny caught the boy by the shoulder before he could run to the bear, which was bawling and snapping at the chain.

   Hal Borland, *When the Legends Die*

Imitations:

A. Quietly, Shea took herself to the side of the playground, holding her candy in her pocket.

B. Near him in the line, he could hear the crying kid, who was perhaps his best friend.

C. Everybody went outside but Sharon, the new girl coming from another school.

D. Bucky tossed the baby in the air before the kid could crawl to her mother, who was ranting and raving at the teenager.

E. The lifeguard reached the crowded shallow end after a worried mother yelled to him that there had been an accident.

PRACTICE 6: EXPANDING

There's more than one way to comb your hair, arrange your room, wash your dog, or tease your little brother or sister. There's more than one way to close a sentence. For each sentence add a *word*, then a *phrase*, then a *dependent clause*.

EXAMPLE

Hour after hour he stood there, silent, motionless, [CLOSER GOES HERE].

Word: Hour after hour he stood there, silent, motionless, **waiting**.

Phrase: Hour after hour he stood there, silent, motionless, **with his faithful dog by his side.**

Dependent clause: Hour after hour he stood there, silent, motionless, **because he was afraid that any movement would attract the monster.**

Original sentence: Hour after hour he stood there, silent, motionless, **a shadow carved in ebony and moonlight.**

James V. Marshall, *Walkabout*

---

1. Not daring to turn her head, from a corner of her eye she grew aware of a strange, humped shadow, ^.

   Lloyd Alexander, *The High King*

2. The houses in the outskirts were all exactly alike, ^.

   Madeleine L'Engle, *A Wrinkle in Time*

3. Another jagged bolt of lightning stretched across the sky, ^.

   R. L. Stine, *Ghost Beach*

4. When he spoke, there appeared before him a giant, ^.

   Walter Dean Myers, *Legend of Tarik*

5. Our teacher Miss Ellis flinched at the pop of Gilly's gum but continued to talk in her calm, professional voice, ^.

   Katherine Paterson, *The Great Gilly Hopkins*

STORY GRAMMAR

Using one of the authors' sentences as a starter sentence, write the opening paragraph of a story. The complete story will take lots of pages to tell, but your job is to write just the first paragraph, at least five sentences long. Write your sentences so well that the author of your starter sentence would say, "Great job!"

- Just as the authors' sentences use closers, within your paragraph use *closers and other sentence-composing tools to make your paragraph sparkle and shine*. For your closers, use at least one word, one phrase, one dependent clause as tools.

- Exchange your rough draft with drafts of other students in your class to get suggestions for improvement. Use suggestions to revise your paragraph to make it better.

- Publish your writing by reading your paragraph to the class or posting it online. See how other students who used your same first sentence wrote their first paragraphs to begin that long story.

Closers Are **Bold:**

1. He waited, **gnawing at his thumbnail.**

    Thomas Rockwell, *How to Eat Fried Worms*

2. We all remembered someone, and I remembered my father, **so tall and strong and kind.**

    Scott O'Dell, *Island of the Blue Dolphins*

3. They were just little kids then, **running away from older boys, like Major, who tried to hold them up for nickels on the street.**

    Robert Lipsyte, *The Contender*

4. The coldness deepened and swirled all about her and through her, and was filled with a new and strange kind of darkness, **a thing that wanted to eat and digest her like some enormous malignant beast of prey.**

    Madeleine L'Engle, *A Wrinkle in Time*

5. He was thin and sunburned, **this wonderful boy, with a thick mop of curly brown hair,** and he wore his battered trousers and loose, grubby shirt with much self-assurance, **as if they were silk and satin.** *(Two sentences joined into one by a comma plus* and. *Both have closers.)*

    Natalie Babbitt, *Tuck Everlasting*

Tip for Better Revising: Always, when you revise something you've written, look for places to use closers plus other sentence-composing tools to add detail and dazzle to your writing.

Review: A closer is a word, phrase, or dependent clause that ends a sentence.

Preview: Get ready to review everything you've learned about sentence positions by playing with sentences from the last book in Lemony Snicket's series, *A Series of Unfortunate Events: The End*.

Reviewing Sentence Positions

A Series of Unfortunate Events: The End by Lemony Snicket

The Last Snickety Story

Lemony Snicket wrote a series of thirteen novels called *A Series of Unfortunate Events*. The first novel is called *The Bad Beginning*, which you read about on page 37. The thirteenth and final book called *The End* begins like this:

If you have ever peeled an onion, then you know that the first thin, papery layer reveals another thin, papery layer, and that layer reveals another, and another, and before you know it you have hundreds of layers all over the kitchen table and thousands of tears in your eyes, sorry that you ever started peeling in the first place and wishing that you had left the onion alone to wither away on the shelf of the pantry while you went on with your life, even if that meant never again enjoying the complicated and overwhelming taste of this strange and bitter vegetable.

In this way, the story of the Baudelaire orphans is like an onion, and if you insist on reading each and every thin, papery layer in *A Series of Unfortunate Events*, your only reward will be 170 chapters of misery in your library and countless tears in your eyes. Even if you have read the first twelve volumes of the Baudelaires' story, it is not too late to stop peeling away the layers and to put this book back on the shelf to wither away while you read something less complicated and overwhelming. The end of this unhappy chronicle is like its bad beginning, as each misfortune only reveals another, and another, and another, and only those with the stomach for this strange and bitter tale should venture any farther into the Baudelaire onion. I'm sorry to tell you this, but that is how the story goes.

The Grammar

The author of the miserable events that befall the children is a very good writer whose sentences are built very well. In these activities, you will read many of his sentences from the thirteenth and last book in the series. You'll learn how to imitate Lemony's sentences. Then you'll write your own sentences built like his.

Within their sentences, talented authors like Lemony Snicket use sentence-building tools of all kinds: *word, phrase, dependent clause.* They put those tools in three positions: *opener, S-V split, closer.* You now know what all that means, so in your sentences you can do the same!

REVIEW 1: FINDING LEMONY TOOLS

Find the tools in each Snickety sentence, and tell what it is (*word, phrase, dependent clause*) and where it is (*opener, S-V split, closer*).

Sentences 1–5 contain one tool:

1. Finally, the baby uttered a word.

2. This ring, with its long secret history, was in your home for years, and your parents never mentioned it.

3. His father on some mornings would come into Klaus's room to wake him up and find him asleep, clutching his flashlight in one hand and his book in the other.

4. The snake seemed to be laughing, although perhaps it was just appreciating the youngest child scratching behind its tiny, hooded ears.

5. In the dim glow of the flashlight, the children could not see clearly the expression on his face.

Sentences 6–10 contain two tools:

6. Sighing, she gazed up at the tall mast of the boat, where a tattered sail drooped limply in the still air.

7. To her horror, she found that her vision was becoming blurry, as if the fungus was growing over her eyes.

8. Like all people, the children came across plenty of things that they were unable to explain, from the hypnotism techniques of Dr. Orwell to the breaking of Klaus's heart by a girl named Fiona.

9. Putting down the harpoon gun, Count Olaf began to pick at the tape with his dirt-encrusted fingernails, peeling away at the nameplate to reveal another name underneath.

10. Until the sun set on the rippling horizon of the sea, the Baudelaire orphans sat all afternoon and sipped and wondered what lay at the heart of their sad lives, when every secret, every mystery, and every unfortunate event had been peeled away.

REVIEW 2: PLACING LEMONY TOOLS

Underneath the sentence are tools. Put them into the sentence where they make sense. For each tool, tell what it is (*word, phrase, dependent clause*) and where you placed it (*opener, S-V split, closer*). When you write out the sentence, include commas for pauses.

1. Her father dipped her bare feet in the water of the fountain.

   a. to quiet the little girl in the hot weather
   b. until the little girl was screaming with laughter

2. The Baudelaire children found themselves laughing.

   a. hugging one another in relief
   b. which is a common reaction among people who have narrowly escaped death

3. The Baudelaires hugged the snake.

   a. particularly Sunny
   b. who had a special attachment to the playful reptile

4. The Baudelaires did not believe in magic

   a. actually
   b. although their mother had a nifty card trick she could occasionally be persuaded to perform

5. Violet and Klaus had begun an argument at breakfast.

   a. a long time ago
   b. before Sunny was born
   c. over taking out the garbage

6. Her belly rose and fell with calm, deep breaths.

   a. full and round from her pregnancy
   b. while her hands lay gently on her chest
   c. as if she were comforting herself, or her child

7. The islanders gasped.

   a. realizing that the facilitator's feet were not injured after all
   b. which requires a large intake of breath
   c. a dangerous thing to do if spores of a deadly fungus are in the air

8. The four castaway children did nothing but weep.

   a. for a minute
   b. letting their tears run down their faces and into the sea
   c. which some have said is nothing but a library of all the tears in history

9. A mysterious figure approached.

    a. from the depths of the sea

    b. almost like a question mark

    c. rising out of the water

10. They had just walked around a grand piano.

    a. which was sticking straight out of the ocean

    b. as if it had fallen from the sky

    c. when something caught the Baudelaire eyes

    d. a tiny white figure scurrying toward them

REVIEW 3: WRITING LIKE LEMONY

Copy each model and its imitation. Then write your own imitation of the same model. Afterward, play "The Guess-the-Model Game." Read to the class one of your imitations, and see who can guess its model. *Remember:* Your goal is to write Lemonys, not lemons!

Model Sentences:

1. Violet, Klaus, and Sunny, like all children, always wanted to believe the best about their parents.

2. At night, when people are sitting upright in bed, having been awakened by a sudden loud noise, they believe in all sorts of supernatural things.

3. Violet picked up an item that lay at her feet, a pink ribbon decorated with plastic daisies, and began to wind it around her hair.

4. I can see her now, sitting on a small couch she used to keep in the corner of her bedroom, adjusting the straps of her sandals with one hand and munching on an apple with the other.

5. At the sound of Sunny's voice, Count Olaf blinked and sat up, glaring at the children and shaking water out of his ears.

Imitations:

A. I can picture her then, standing in a sunlit kitchen she used to visit in the quiet of the morning, opening the door of the refrigerator with one hand and pulling out the milk with the other.

B. On a bench on the boardwalk, the kid sat and glanced around, staring at the bicyclists and thinking sadly about his accident.

C. Chrissy, Carla, and Cindy, like all sisters, wanted to receive the most for their birthday.

D. The raven pecked at a seed that lay near the garden, a watermelon seed left from the picnic, and started to open it with its beak.

E. In time, when students are remembering thoughtfully about schooling, having been educated by some warm, skillful teachers, they realize all kinds of important lessons.

REVIEW 4: RETOOLING SNICKETY SENTENCES

Variety is the spice of life, so spice up some sentences. Here's how. The sentences below lack variety because the Lemony tools—with a lemon zest spice—have been removed. Add spicy tools to each of the Snickety sentences, using a zesty imagination like Lemony's.

Add Openers—Some Words, Some Phrases, Some Dependent Clauses:

1. ^, the baby uttered a word.

2. ^, the children could hear the sound of approaching thunder.

3. ^, she gazed up at the tall mast of the boat, where a tattered sail drooped limply in the still air.

4. ^, the youngest Baudelaire was peering into the jar.

5. *(Add two openers.)* ^, ^, the Baudelaire orphans wondered about their own unfortunate history, and that of their parents and all the other castaways who had washed up on the shores of the island.

Add S-V Splits—Some Words, Some Phrases, Some Dependent Clauses:

6. Willa, ^, decided against a garden hose that was encrusted with barnacles.

7. A navigational compass, ^, is made from a small piece of magnetized metal and a simple pivot.

8. Byam, ^, discarded some batteries he had found.

9. The girl, ^, howled and howled.

10. The baby clutching the boat, ^, would soon vanish from this chronicle.

Add Closers—Some Words, Some Phrases, Some Dependent Clauses:

11. She lived with her siblings in a house owned by a terrible woman, ^.

12. Count Olaf stood proudly at the front of the boat, ^.

13. *(Add two closers.)* Count Olaf led the way, ^ and ^.

14. *(Add two closers.)* The three children looked at one another, ^ and ^.

15. *(Add two closers.)* The Baudelaire children hugged the snake, ^, ^.

Building Better Sentences

The paragraph below is based upon an incident in Lemony Snicket's *The End*: the three orphaned Baudelaire children follow the trail of a huge but friendly snake to a secret cavern hidden under a tree. The sentences in the paragraph are ordinary, without detail or variety. You can make them much, much better.

Here's how. Each sentence at the caret marks (^) has places for you to add tools to make each sentence more interesting and well written, like the sentences in Lemony Snicket's story. For your tools, use variety (the spice of life)—a word, a phrase, or a dependent clause, or some of each. Spice them up with Lemony zest!

"The Secret Cavern Under the Tree"

1. ^, the huge but friendly snake slithered away from the children, ^.

2. ^ Sunny, the youngest of the three children, followed her beloved snake.

3. ^, Violet and Klaus, the other two Baudelaire children, ^, followed Sunny.

4. The children discovered footprints, ^.

5. The footprints led to the apple tree, ^.

6. The children, ^, caught sight of the friendly snake as it disappeared through a hole in the tree's roots.

7. ^, they followed after the friendly snake to enter the huge opening in the tree's roots, ^.

8. ^ , they realized they were standing in a large underground cavern, where they could safely hide, ^.

9. Inside this cavern, ^, were amazing items, such as ^, ^, ^, and ^.

10. The children, ^, gave big squeals of delight as the friendly snake, ^, made a loud hiss of happiness.

"LAURELS"

Having done a spectacular job learning how to build better sentences like those of famous authors like Lemony Snicket and many, many others, you're almost finished. Here's how Lemony Snicket might put it: "Don't rest on your laurels."

You may wish to know what that expression means—or you may not, but you're going to learn anyway because you might be asked on a quiz show with a gazillion-dollar prize to explain it, and all the other contestants, upon hearing the question, will lower their chins to their chests in dismay (a word meaning "disappointment" as in "I was dismayed that the bathroom was occupied").

From ancient times, leaves of laurels were woven into wreaths, then placed as crowns on the heads of really good writers (or athletes) or athletic writers or literary athletes to honor their stellar achievements. (The word *stellar* means "high," as in "stars are stellar because they're high in the sky"). Some of those so honored would then stop trying any more (to write, to run, to jump, to hurl their bodies through midair to see how far they could fling their flesh). They were ultra tired and super weary, completely and understandably exhausted from hurling their entire heavy flesh long distances. When it was all over, and atop their head was placed a crown of laurel wreath, they just wanted to rest on their stellar achievements: their laurels. Hence, the expression "resting on your laurels." Don't.

P.S. This abbreviation means "postscript," from *after* (post) and from *the writing* (script), as in "Hoping to get a part in the school play, I rehearsed by reading the script (that is, the words written for the play's characters to speak on stage) over and over *ad infinitum*," which is a Latin expression meaning "to infinity," "infinity" meaning "forever," like this sentence, which has gone on *ad infinitum*—or, more accurately, *ad nauseam*, an expression too disgusting to explain here, especially because it might be around lunchtime where you are. However, if you are insatiably curious, you'll look it up. While you're at it, also look up *insatiably*.

Here's the long-delayed P.S. This book is called *Story Grammar* for a good reason. You've read hundreds of sentences from famous stories and practiced how to write your own story sentences. Now, *without resting on your laurels*, you are going to write a complete story!

You now know why it is absolutely and definitely *not* okay to rest on your laurels.

You may wonder, though, is there no rest for the weary? Well, yes. there is. If you're tired, you can rest on something soft, just not your laurels, which anyway have the texture of tacos and therefore make for very uncomfortable resting. Cots, hammocks, sofas, beaches, bellies of brown bears, and best of all, beds—all of them make suitable resting places. If you choose bear belly, first make sure the bear is sleeping, soundly, or preferably dead, freshly.

Okay, tonight, on a comfy bed, not a bear's belly, living or dead, get a good night's rest so you'll be crisp as a potato chip, alert as an ant in the path of rampaging elephants, ready to start your very own *Harry Potter* story—after which, you may rest, on anything, including laurels.

Good night, sleep tight, and don't let the bedbugs bite. Actually, don't even let them into your bed—unless you need some bugs for science class.

R-r-r-r-r-i-n-g! Alarm clock! Time to get up and get moving on your story. Think laurels.

Preview: Now you know lots of sentence-building tools and places to put them in your sentences. J. K. Rowling also knows all of that and builds sentences magically with all the tools and positions in her seven famous *Harry Potter* stories.

In the next and last section of this worktext, you'll learn how J. K. Rowling creates those magic sentences. Then you'll conjure up everything you've learned to compose your own magic sentences for your *Harry Potter* story (a few pages long, not *ad infinitum*, with hundreds and hundreds and hundreds of pages like Rowling's), brewed from the same sentence potions she concocts.

In this final activity of *Story Grammar*, you will write an original episode for the *Harry Potter* story with your own sentences built much like the sentences of J. K. Rowling, a powerful sentence builder.

What's An Episode?

An episode is an important part of a long story. The *Harry Potter* novels tell a very long story, occupying approximately five thousand pages containing hundreds of fascinating, memorable episodes. That's a lot of sentence building! (Don't worry. Yours won't be nearly that long, not even close. Now relax.)

Write an episode of several paragraphs featuring a new character for the *Harry Potter* story. Your new character can be good (like Hagrid, Harry's huge protector, a gentle giant of a man) or evil (like Voldemort, Harry's constant pursuer, a hideous but powerful demon bent on killing Harry). Give your character a memorable unusual name, a name similar to *Hagrid* or *Voldemort*.

If you choose a good character, show that character defending Harry in a dangerous situation. If you chose an evil character, show that character threatening Harry in a horrifying situation.

As you think about what character to create, listen to how J. K. Rowling, the author of the *Harry Potter* novels, came up with Harry. Hard thinking comes before good writing. J. K. Rowling thought long and hard about the idea before she actually began writing:

> When I was traveling back to London on my own on a crowded train, the idea for Harry Potter simply fell into my head. I had been writing almost continuously since the age of six but I had never been so excited about an idea before. To my immense frustration, I didn't have a functioning pen with me, and I was too shy to ask anybody if I could borrow one. I think, now, that this was probably a good thing, because I simply sat and thought, for four (delayed train) hours, and all the details bubbled up in my brain, and this scrawny, black-haired, bespectacled boy who didn't know he was a wizard became more and more real to me. (From J. K. Rowling's official website)

Using J. K. Rowling's writing style, write your episode about an exciting incident featuring the new good or evil character, written so well that your readers will think it was written by J. K. Rowling herself!

In several paragraphs, tell the story of what happens when your good character saves Harry Potter from a very dangerous situation or your evil character threatens

Harry Potter in a horrifying situation. To help plan your episode, jot down answers to the following questions.

Planning Your Episode
(Prewriting)

Setting is where the episode takes place.

1. In what place or places does the situation happen? How do Harry Potter and your new character happen to be there?

2. What time of day is it? Is the atmosphere peaceful, happy, pleasant or gloomy, scary, tense, mysterious?

Characters are the people, creatures, monsters, spirits, muggles, witches, wizards, and Hogwarts students included in your episode.

3. What does your main character look like, and how is he or she dressed?

4. What is your main character's name?

5. What quality of your main character will you emphasize? Here are some possibilities for a good character: *bravery, honesty, courage, loyalty, devotion, kindness, self-sacrifice.* Here are some possibilities for an evil character: *wickedness, ugliness, meanness, anger, cruelty, deceitfulness, brutality.*

6. What other characters will you invent for your episode? What characters from the *Harry Potter* stories, if any, will you include?

Plot is what happens in your episode, including incidents, scenes, and other important events.

7. How will your episode begin, and how will it end?

8. What will be the main happening in your episode, the incident you spend the most time planning and writing because it should be the most memorable part of your story?

Potterisms are aspects of the actual *Harry Potter* story that author J. K. Rowling uses frequently.

9. What are some creatures, places, characters, monsters and demons, magical objects, languages, spells, and charms from *Harry Potter* stories (books or

movies) that you want to include in your episode? *Examples:* Fluffy the Three-Headed Dog, Dementors, Bogart Wardrobe, Scabbers the Rat, Buckbeak, Nagini the Snake, The Vanishing Cabinet, Felix Felicis, Merpeople, Dobby, Thestral, Mountain Troll, Hippogriff, Doxy.

10. What are some names of persons, places, or things from *Harry Potter* stories (books or movies) that you want to include in your episode? *Examples:* (persons) Ron, Hermione, Hagrid, Dumbledore, Voldemort, Professor Snape; (places) Hogwarts School of Witchcraft and Wizardry, Diagon Alley, Privet Drive; (things) The Invisibility Cloak, The Sorting Hat, Mirror of Erised, Polyjuice Potion.

Title is the attention-getting name of your episode. Yours will be *Harry Potter and the*—what?

11. What part of your episode will the title come from?

12. What are some good titles you will choose from?

Revision is rewriting the episode to improve it.

13. How will you get help from other people to make the writing better?

14. How will you help yourself to make the writing better?

Editing is the last step in revising to make sure your episode is ready to be given to readers.

15. How will you make sure that your last revision uses good spelling and grammar and looks attractive?

Publication is sharing your writing with others for them to enjoy.

16. What are some ways—at school, at home, online, or elsewhere—you'll show your episode to others for them to enjoy?

Listen to J. K. Rowling's excitement when, after years of trying to find a publisher, her agent Christopher called her to tell her the terrific news that her book, the first *Harry Potter* novel, finally would be published:

It took a year for my new agent, Christopher, to find a publisher. Lots of them turned it down. Then, finally, in August 1996, Christopher telephoned me and told me that Bloomsbury had "made an offer." I could not quite believe my ears. "You mean it's going to be published?" I asked, rather stupidly. "It's definitely going to be published?" After I had hung up, I screamed and jumped into the air; Jessica [her baby daughter], who was sitting in her high-chair enjoying tea, looked thoroughly scared. And you probably know what happened next. (From J. K. Rowling's official website)

Yes, the whole world knows what happened next: the biggest series of best-selling books ever! Maybe, one day, like author J. K. Rowling, you'll get a book published! Get excited! Start by writing a terrific *Harry Potter* episode that everyone will want to read!

Requirements: Sentence-Composing Tools

- *Imitations:* Include within your episode *three imitations* of any of the model sentences on pages 95–99. Hide them inside your episode so readers can't guess which sentences are imitations. They'll be hidden if all of your sentences, not just the imitations, are built well.

- *Tools:* Use frequently the *words, phrases, dependent clauses* you learned in this worktext. Make some tools short (one to five words), some medium (six to ten words), some long (eleven or more words).

- *Positions:* Put tools in different positions: *openers, S-V splits, closers*. Sometimes, within the same sentence, use two or all three positions.

- *Multiple tools:* Occasionally, within the same sentence, use more than one of the same kind of tool. (See page 98 for examples.)

- *Mixed tools:* Sometimes, within the same sentence use two or more different kinds of tools. (See page 98 for examples.)

The Sentence-Composing Power Tools

Taken from all seven of the *Harry Potter* novels, these model sentences were built by J. K. Rowling with the same power tools you've learned and practiced. Use them to build magical sentences for your own *Harry Potter* episode.

You may choose any three model sentences from the list of thirty-three below to imitate and then include within your episode. *Important:* You must hide your three imitation sentences inside your episode so readers can't tell where they are.

To make sure they are hidden, *all of your sentences—not just the imitation sentences— must be well built, like sentences by author J. K. Rowling.*

As you read these thirty-three sentences, notice how J. K. Rowling uses the sentence-composing tools from this worktext powerfully to build sentences for her seven novels of the *Harry Potter* series. In your *Harry Potter* episode, see how many tools you can include to make your writing similar to hers.

Words as Openers, S-V Splits, and Closers:

1. **Furious**, Harry threw his ingredients and his bag into his cauldron and dragged it up to the front of the dungeon to the empty table.

   Harry Potter and the Goblet of Fire

2. **Slowly**, the snake raised its head until its eyes were on a level with Harry's.

   Harry Potter and the Sorcerer's Stone

3. **Wordlessly**, Dumbledore gestured to Harry to come to his side.

   Harry Potter and the Half-Blood Prince

4. A giant spider, **hairy**, was advancing on Ron.

   Harry Potter and the Prisoner of Azkaban

5. A hundred or so tufty little plants, **purplish**, were growing there in rows.

   Harry Potter and the Chamber of Secrets

6. Bellatrix's face, **flushed**, had turned an ugly, blotchy red.

   Harry Potter and the Deathly Hallows

7. Harry was on his feet again, **furious**.

   Harry Potter and the Order of the Phoenix

8. Justin Finch Fletchley was lying on the floor, **rigid**.

   Harry Potter and the Chamber of Secrets

9. Charlie was shorter than Ron, **thickset**.

   Harry Potter and the Deathly Hallows

Phrases as Openers, S-V Splits, and Closers:

10. **Repulsed by what he was doing**, Harry forced the goblet back toward Dumbledore's mouth and tipped it for Dumbledore to drink the remainder of the horrible potion inside.

     Harry Potter and the Half-Blood Prince

11. **At daybreak on a fine summer's morning**, a maid had entered the drawing room to find all three Riddles dead.

     Harry Potter and the Chamber of Secrets

12. **To make Dudley feel better about eating "rabbit food,"** Aunt Petunia had insisted that the whole family follow the same diet, too.

     Harry Potter and the Goblet of Fire

13. Fudge, **a portly little man in a long, pinstriped cloak**, looked cold and exhausted.

     Harry Potter and the Prisoner of Azkaban

14. Neville, **clutching his wrist**, hobbled off with Madame Hooch.

     Harry Potter and the Sorcerer's Stone

15. The brutal-faced Death Eater, **last to leave the tower top**, was disappearing through the door.

     Harry Potter and the Half-Blood Prince

16. A voice came suddenly out of the shadows, **a soft, misty sort of voice**.

     Harry Potter and the Prisoner of Azkaban

17. Uncle Vernon and Aunt Petunia froze where they stood, **staring at Dudley as though he had just expressed a desire to become a ballerina**.

     Harry Potter and the Deathly Hallows

18. The Fanged Frisbee zoomed around the common room, **attempting to take bites of the tapestry**.

     Harry Potter and the Half-Blood Prince

Dependent Clauses as Openers, S-V Splits, and Closers:

19. **As Harry shivered and drew his robes tightly around him,** he heard what sounded like a thousand fingernails scraping an enormous blackboard.

    Harry Potter and the Chamber of Secrets

20. **Although he could tell it was daylight,** he kept his eyes shut.

    Harry Potter and the Sorcerer's Stone

21. **When Harry got outside again,** he found Ron being violently sick in the pumpkin patch.

    Harry Potter and the Chamber of Secrets

22. Aunt Petunia, **whose face had been buried in her handkerchief,** looked around at the sound.

    Harry Potter and the Deathly Hallows

23. Professor Snape, **who seemed to have attained new levels of vindictiveness over the summer,** gave Neville detention.

    Harry Potter and the Goblet of Fire

24. Harry, **who had not had the heart to tell her that Dobby was taking everything she made,** bent lower over his History of Magic essay.

    Harry Potter and the Order of the Phoenix

25. He glanced at Snape, **whose black eyes glistened.**

    Harry Potter and the Chamber of Secrets

26. He raised the wand above his head and brought it swishing down through the dusty air **as a stream of red and gold sparks shot from the end like a firework.**

    Harry Potter and the Sorcerer's Stone

27. The first thing they saw was Peeves the Poltergeist, **who was floating upside down in midair and stuffing the nearest keyhole with chewing gum.**

    Harry Potter and the Prisoner of Azkaban

Multiple Tools

For your *Harry Potter* episode, include within some sentences *two or more of the same kind of tool,* like an ice-cream cone with two or even more dips of chocolate instead of just one dip.

28. *Multiple words:* **Puzzled** but **interested**, the class got to its feet and followed Professor Lupin out of the classroom. *(two words)*

    Harry Potter and the Prisoner of Azkaban

29. *Multiple phrases:* **Blinded by the blaze of the spells blasting from every direction, deafened by a series of bangs, terrified by it all**, Harry blinked and looked down at the floor. *(three phrases)*

    Harry Potter and the Goblet of Fire

30. *Multiple dependent clauses:* **As he soared upward, as the wind rushed through his hair, as the crowd's faces became mere flesh-colored pinpricks below, and as the Horntail shrank to the size of a dog**, he realized that he had left not only the ground behind, but also his fear. *(four dependent clauses)*

    Harry Potter and the Goblet of Fire

Mixed Tools

For your *Harry Potter* episode, also include within some sentences *two or more different kinds of tools,* like an ice-cream cone with one dip of chocolate, another dip of strawberry—or even more flavors—instead of just one flavor.

31. He had been down at Hagrid's hut, **helping him feed Norbert, who was now eating dead rats by the crate.** *(one phrase, one dependent clause)*

    Harry Potter and the Sorcerer's Stone

32. **Dizzy, bruised, covered in soot**, Harry got gingerly to his feet, **holding his broken glasses up to his eyes.** *(two words, two phrases)*

    Harry Potter and the Chamber of Secrets

33. As they drew nearer to the silhouetted figure at the table, Voldemort's face shone through the gloom, **hairless, snakelike, with slits for nostrils and gleaming red eyes, whose pupils were vertical.** *(two words, one phrase, one dependent clause)*

Harry Potter and the Deathly Hallows

These are the powerful sentence builders, your invisible teachers whose lessons for you are the sentences they built. You've read their great sentences and learned and practiced their great grammar. By using this list to make selections, read some of their great stories.

Here's a complete list of their names and stories from which their sentences came, a library of terrific reading, with, for sure, well-built sentences. Read some of these terrific tales over vacation time in winter, spring, or summer or anytime. They make good reading and can also help you become a good writer like J. K. Rowling.

Asked her advice for young people who want to write, J. K. Rowling, author of the *Harry Potter* novels, said, "The most important thing is to read as much as you can, like I did. It will give you an understanding of what makes good writing, and it will enlarge your vocabulary. And it's a lot of fun!"

Read often and pay attention to good sentences. Write lots of them. Have fun.

Your Invisible Teachers: The Powerful Sentence Builders

Armstrong Sperry, *Call It Courage*

Arnold Lobel, *Frog and Toad Are Friends*

Arthur C. Clarke, *Dolphin Island*

Betsy Byars, *The Summer of the Swans*

Beverly Cleary, *Dear Mr. Henshaw*

Beverly Cleary, *The Mouse and the Motorcycle*

Beverly Cleary, *Ramona the Brave*

Beverly Cleary, *Ramona and Her Father*

Beverly Cleary, *Ramona Forever*

Beverly Cleary, *Ramona the Pest*

Bill and Vera Cleaver, *Where the Lilies Bloom*

C. S. Lewis, *The Chronicles of Narnia: The Lion, the Witch, and the Wardrobe*

C. S. Lewis, *The Chronicles of Narnia: Prince Caspian*

Carl Hiaasen, *Flush*

Carl Hiaasen, *Hoot*

Carolyn Keene, *Nancy Drew: The Bungalow Mystery*

Carolyn Keene, *Nancy Drew: The Mystery at Lilac Inn*

Charles Portis, *True Grit*

Chris Van Allsburg, *The Sweetest Fig*

Christopher Paolini, *Eragon*

Christopher Paul Curtis, *Bud, Not Buddy*

Cynthia Rylant, *Missing May*

Cynthia Voigt, *Homecoming*

Deborah and James Howe, *Bunnicula: A Rabbit-Tale of Mystery*

Donna Hill, "Ghost Cat"

E. B. White, *Charlotte's Web*

E. B. White, *Stuart Little*

E. B. White, *The Trumpet of the Swan*

E. L. Konigsburg, *From the Mixed-up Files of Mrs. Basil E. Frankweiler*

Edmund Ware, "An Underground Episode"

Eleanor Coerr, *Sadako and the Thousand Paper Cranes*

Elinor Mordaunt, "The Prince and the Goose Girl"

Elizabeth Coatsworth, "The Story of Wang Li"

Elizabeth George Speare, *The Witch of Blackbird Pond*

Emily Neville, *It's Like This, Cat*

Frances Hodgson Burnett, *A Little Princess*

Frances Hodgson Burnett, *The Secret Garden*

Frank Bonham, *Chief*

Franklin W. Dixon, *The Hardy Boys: The House on the Cliff*

Franklin W. Dixon, *The Hardy Boys: The Secret of the Old Mill*

Franklin W. Dixon, *The Hardy Boys: The Tower Treasure*

Fred Gipson, *Old Yeller*

Gail Carson Levine, *Ella Enchanted*

Gary Paulsen, *Hatchet*

Gary Paulsen, *The Tent*

Gary Paulsen, *The Time Hackers*

Hal Borland, *When the Legends Die*

Hans Augusto Rey, *Curious George*

Harry Allard, *Miss Nelson Is Missing!*

Henry Gregor Felsen, "Horatio"

J. K. Rowling, *Harry Potter and the Chamber of Secrets*

J. K. Rowling, *Harry Potter and the Deathly Hallows*

J. K. Rowling, *Harry Potter and the Goblet of Fire*

J. K. Rowling, *Harry Potter and the Half-Blood Prince*

J. K. Rowling, *Harry Potter and the Order of the Phoenix*

J. K. Rowling, *Harry Potter and the Prisoner of Azkaban*

J. K. Rowling, *Harry Potter and the Sorcerer's Stone*

J. M. Coetzee, *Life and Times of Michael K*

J. R. R. Tolkien, *The Hobbit*

J. R. R. Tolkien, *The Lord of the Rings: The Fellowship of the Ring*

Jack London, *The Call of the Wild*

Jack Prelutsky, "A Day at the Zoo"

James Howe, *Bunnicula: The Celery Stalks at Midnight*

James Howe, *Bunnicula Strikes Again!*

James V. Marshall, *Walkabout*

Jean Craighead George, *Julie of the Wolves*

Jean Fritz, *Homesick: My Own Story*

Jean Merrill, *The Pushcart War*

Jeanne Birdsall, *The Penderwicks*

Jerry Spinelli, *Maniac Magee*

Johanna Spyri, *Heidi*

John Christopher, *The Guardians*

John Clarke, "The Boy Who Painted Christ Black"

John Steinbeck, *The Red Pony*

Joseph Krumgold, *Onion John*

Judy Blume, *Here's to You, Rachel Robinson*

Judy Blume, *Tales of a Fourth Grade Nothing*

K. A. Applegate, *Animorphs: The Underground*

Kate DiCamillo, *Because of Winn-Dixie*

Kate DiCamillo, *The Miraculous Journey of Edward Tulane*

Kate DiCamillo, *The Tiger Rising*

Katherine Paterson, *Bridge to Terabithia*

Katherine Paterson, *The Great Gilly Hopkins*

Katherine Paterson, *Jacob Have I Loved*

Katherine Paterson, *Park's Quest*

Kenneth Grahame, *The Wind in the Willows*

L. M. Montgomery, *Anne of Green Gables*

Larry Weinberg, *Ghost Hotel*

Lauren St. John, *The White Giraffe*

Laurence Yep, *Dragonwings*

Lemony Snicket, *A Series of Unfortunate Events: The Bad Beginning*

Lemony Snicket, *A Series of Unfortunate Events: The End*

Leo Lionni, "Swimmy"

Leon Hugo, "My Father and the Hippopotamus"

Lloyd Alexander, *The Book of Three*

Lloyd Alexander, *The High King*

Lois Lowry, *The Giver*

Louis Sachar, *Holes*

Louis Sachar, *There's a Boy in the Girls' Bathroom*

Louisa May Alcott, "Onawandah"

Louise Fitzhugh, *Harriet the Spy*

Lynne Reid Banks, *The Indian in the Cupboard*

Lynne Reid Banks, *One More River*

Madeleine L'Engle, *A Swiftly Tilting Planet*

Madeleine L'Engle, *A Wrinkle in Time*

Maia Wojciechowska, *Shadow of a Bull*

Margery Williams, *The Velveteen Rabbit*

Marguerite Henry, *Misty of Chincoteague*

Marjorie Kinnan Rawlings, *The Yearling*

Mary O'Hara, *My Friend Flicka*

Mercer Mayer, "There's a Nightmare in My Closet"

Mildred D. Taylor, *Let the Circle Be Unbroken*

Mildred D. Taylor, *Roll of Thunder, Hear My Cry*

Mildred D. Taylor, *Song of the Trees*

N. B. Grace, *High School Musical: The Junior Novel*

Natalie Babbitt, *Tuck Everlasting*

Norah Burke, "Polar Night"

Patricia C. McKissack, "A Million Fish, More or Less"

Patricia MacLachland, *Sarah, Plain and Tall*

Phyllis Reynolds Naylor, *Shiloh*

Post Wheeler, "Vasilissa the Beautiful"

R. L. Stine, *Ghost Beach*

Ray Bradbury, "I See You Never"

Ray Bradbury, "A Sound of Thunder"

Ray Bradbury, "The Whole Town's Sleeping"

Richard Bach, *Jonathan Livingston Seagull*

Richard E. Byrd, *Alone*

Roald Dahl, *The BFG*

Roald Dahl, *Charlie and the Chocolate Factory*

Roald Dahl, *Fantastic Mr. Fox*

Roald Dahl, *James and the Giant Peach*

Roald Dahl, *Matilda*

Robb White, *Deathwatch*

Robert C. O'Brien, *Mrs. Frisby and the Rats of NIMH*

Robert Lipsyte, *The Brave*

Robert Lipsyte, *The Contender*

Robert McCloskey, "Make Way for Ducklings"

Roger Duvoisin, "Petunia"

Rosa Guy, *Edith Jackson*

Rosa Guy, *The Friends*

Rudyard Kipling, *The Jungle Book*

Sam McBratney, "Guess How Much I Love You"

Scott O'Dell, *Island of the Blue Dolphins*

Sid Fleischman, *The Whipping Boy*

Susan Patron, *The Higher Power of Lucky*

Theodore Taylor, *The Cay*

Thomas Rockwell, *How to Eat Fried Worms*

Walter Dean Myers, *Legend of Tarik*

Walter Dean Myers, *Motown and Didi*

Wanda Gag, "Millions of Cats"

William Barrett, *The Lilies of the Field*

William Faulkner, "A Rose for Emily"

William H. Armstrong, *Sounder*

William Steig, "Sylvester and the Magic Pebble"

Wilson Rawls, *Where the Red Fern Grows*

Winifred Finlay, "The Water-Horse of Barra"

Your Invisible Teachers: The Stories Their Sentences Built

Here are two lists of stories used in *Story Grammar for Elementary School*. The titles of short stories are in quotation marks and the titles of long stories are in italics.

Short Stories:

"A Day at the Zoo" by Jack Prelutsky

"A Million Fish, More or Less" by Patricia C. McKissack

"A Rose for Emily" by William Faulkner

"A Sound of Thunder" by Ray Bradbury

"An Underground Episode" by Edmund Ware

"Ghost Cat" by Donna Hill

"Guess How Much I Love You" by Sam McBratney

"Horatio" by Henry Gregor Felsen

"I See You Never" by Ray Bradbury

"Make Way for Ducklings" by Robert McCloskey

"Millions of Cats" by Wanda Gag

"My Father and the Hippopotamus" by Leon Hugo

"Onawandah" by Louisa May Alcott

"Petunia" by Roger Duvoisin

"Polar Night" by Norah Burke

"Swimmy" by Leo Lionni

"Sylvester and the Magic Pebble" by William Steig

"The Boy Who Painted Christ Black" by John Clarke

"The Prince and the Goose Girl" by Elinor Mordaunt

"The Story of Wang Li" by Elizabeth Coatsworth

"The Water-Horse of Barra" by Winifred Finlay

"The Whole Town's Sleeping" by Ray Bradbury

"There's a Nightmare in My Closet" by Mercer Mayer

"Vasilissa the Beautiful" by Post Wheeler

Long Stories:

A Little Princess by Frances Hodgson Burnett

A Series of Unfortunate Events: The Bad Beginning by Lemony Snicket

A Series of Unfortunate Events: The End by Lemony Snicket

A Swiftly Tilting Planet by Madeleine L'Engle

A Wrinkle in Time by Madeleine L'Engle

Alone by Richard E. Byrd

Animorphs: The Underground by K. A. Applegate

Anne of Green Gables by L. M. Montgomery

Because of Winn-Dixie by Kate DiCamillo

Bridge to Terabithia by Katherine Paterson

Bud, Not Buddy by Christopher Paul Curtis

Bunnicula: The Celery Stalks at Midnight by James Howe

Bunnicula: A Rabbit-Tale of Mystery by Deborah and James Howe

Bunnicula Strikes Again! by James Howe

Call It Courage by Armstrong Sperry

Charlie and the Chocolate Factory by Roald Dahl

Charlotte's Web by E. B. White

Chief by Frank Bonham

Curious George by Hans Augusto Rey

Dear Mr. Henshaw by Beverly Cleary

Deathwatch by Robb White

Dolphin Island by Arthur C. Clarke

Dragonwings by Laurence Yep

Edith Jackson by Rosa Guy

Ella Enchanted by Gail Carson Levine

Eragon by Christopher Paolini

Fantastic Mr. Fox by Roald Dahl

Flush by Carl Hiaasen

Frog and Toad Are Friends by Arnold Lobel

From the Mixed-up Files of Mrs. Basil E. Frankweiler by E. L. Konigsburg

Ghost Beach by R. L. Stine

Ghost Hotel by Larry Weinberg

Harriet the Spy by Louise Fitzhugh

Harry Potter and the Chamber of Secrets by J. K. Rowling

Harry Potter and the Deathly Hallows by J. K. Rowling

Harry Potter and the Goblet of Fire by J. K. Rowling

Harry Potter and the Half-Blood Prince by J. K. Rowling

Harry Potter and the Order of the Phoenix by J. K. Rowling

Harry Potter and the Prisoner of Azkaban by J. K. Rowling

Harry Potter and the Sorcerer's Stone by J. K. Rowling

Hatchet by Gary Paulsen

Heidi by Johanna Spyri

Here's to You, Rachel Robinson by Judy Blume

High School Musical: The Junior Novel by N. B. Grace

Holes by Louis Sachar

Homecoming by Cynthia Voigt

Homesick: My Own Story by Jean Fritz

Hoot by Carl Hiaasen

How to Eat Fried Worms by Thomas Rockwell

Island of the Blue Dolphins by Scott O'Dell

It's Like This, Cat by Emily Neville

Jacob Have I Loved by Katherine Paterson

James and the Giant Peach by Roald Dahl

Jonathan Livingston Seagull by Richard Bach

Julie of the Wolves by Jean Craighead George

Legend of Tarik by Walter Dean Myers

Let the Circle Be Unbroken by Mildred D. Taylor

Life and Times of Michael K by J. M. Coetzee

Maniac Magee by Jerry Spinelli

Matilda by Roald Dahl

Miss Nelson Is Missing! by Harry Allard

Missing May by Cynthia Rylant

Misty of Chincoteague by Marguerite Henry

Motown and Didi by Walter Dean Myers

Mrs. Frisby and the Rats of NIMH by Robert C. O'Brien

My Friend Flicka by Mary O'Hara

Nancy Drew: The Bungalow Mystery by Carolyn Keene

Nancy Drew: The Mystery at Lilac Inn by Carolyn Keene

Old Yeller by Fred Gipson

One More River by Lynne Reid Banks

Onion John by Joseph Krumgold

Park's Quest by Katherine Paterson

Ramona and Her Father by Beverly Cleary

Ramona Forever by Beverly Cleary

Ramona the Brave by Beverly Cleary

Ramona the Pest by Beverly Cleary

Roll of Thunder, Hear My Cry by Mildred D. Taylor

Sadako and the Thousand Paper Cranes by Eleanor Coerr

Sarah, Plain and Tall by Patricia MacLachland

Shadow of a Bull by Maia Wojciechowska

Shiloh by Phyllis Reynolds Naylor

Song of the Trees by Mildred D. Taylor

Sounder by William H. Armstrong

Stuart Little by E. B. White

Tales of a Fourth Grade Nothing by Judy Blume

The BFG by Roald Dahl

The Book of Three by Lloyd Alexander

The Brave by Robert Lipsyte

The Call of the Wild by Jack London

The Cay by Theodore Taylor

The Chronicles of Narnia: The Lion, the Witch, and the Wardrobe by C. S. Lewis

The Chronicles of Narnia: Prince Caspian by C. S. Lewis

The Contender by Robert Lipsyte

The Friends by Rosa Guy

The Giver by Lois Lowry

The Great Gilly Hopkins by Katherine Paterson

The Guardians by John Christopher

The Hardy Boys: The House on the Cliff by Franklin W. Dixon

The Hardy Boys: The Secret of the Old Mill by Franklin W. Dixon

The Hardy Boys: The Tower Treasure by Franklin W. Dixon

The High King by Lloyd Alexander

The Higher Power of Lucky by Susan Patron

The Hobbit by J. R. R. Tolkien

The Indian in the Cupboard by Lynne Reid Banks

The Jungle Book by Rudyard Kipling

The Lilies of the Field by William Barrett

The Lord of the Rings: The Fellowship of the Ring by J. R. R. Tolkien

The Miraculous Journey of Edward Tulane by Kate DiCamillo

The Mouse and the Motorcycle by Beverly Cleary

The Penderwicks by Jeanne Birdsall

The Pushcart War by Jean Merrill

The Red Pony by John Steinbeck

The Secret Garden by Frances Hodgson Burnett

The Summer of the Swans by Betsy Byars

The Sweetest Fig by Chris Van Allsburg

The Tent by Gary Paulsen

The Tiger Rising by Kate DiCamillo

The Time Hackers by Gary Paulsen

The Trumpet of the Swan by E. B. White

The Velveteen Rabbit by Margery Williams

The Whipping Boy by Sid Fleischman

The White Giraffe by Lauren St. John

The Wind in the Willows by Kenneth Grahame

The Witch of Blackbird Pond by Elizabeth George Speare

The Yearling by Marjorie Kinnan Rawlings

There's a Boy in the Girls' Bathroom by Louis Sachar

True Grit by Charles Portis

Tuck Everlasting by Natalie Babbitt

Walkabout by James V. Marshall

When the Legends Die by Hal Borland

Where the Lilies Bloom by Bill and Vera Cleaver

Where the Red Fern Grows by Wilson Rawls

We hope that for you, *Story Grammar for Elementary School* had a good beginning (*opener*), middle (*S-V split*), and, of course, a happy ending (*closer*).

Now it's time to say good-bye. At the beginning of *The End,* Lemony Snicket laments, "I'm sorry to tell you this, but that is how the story [grammar] goes." (The word *laments* means "uttered with regret and sadness." The word *uttered* means "said." The word *word* means, of course, "word." All of it means this: Lemony—and we—feel very sad that it's ending.)

> Since my childhood feels like a story, I decided to tell it that way, letting the events fall as they would into the shape of a story.
>
> Jean Fritz, *Homesick: My Own Story*

Use your story grammar for everything you write, maybe even writing your own story, "letting the events fall as they would into the shape of a story." If you do, we hope that it has a—

HAPPY ENDING!